CW01582324

Pies or Pie Charts?

Astonishingly simple recipes to outthink, outpace and outmanoeuvre your competition

John Acton

ISBN: 978-1-914151-57-6

Published by:
The Endless Bookcase
Suite 14, STANTA Business Centre, 3 Soothouse Spring, St Albans, Hertfordshire, UK, AL3 6PF.
www.theendlessbookcase.com

Paperback Edition:
Also available in multiple ebook formats.

Copyright © 2025 John Acton
All rights reserved. No part of this publication may be reproduced, stored or transmitted in any form or by any means, electronic, mechanical, photocopying, recording, scanning, or otherwise without written permission from the publisher. It is illegal to copy this book, post it to a website, or distribute it by any other means without permission.
John Acton has no responsibility for the persistence or accuracy of URLs for external or third-party Internet Websites referred to in this publication and does not guarantee that any content on such Websites is, or will remain, accurate or appropriate.
Designations used by companies to distinguish their products are often claimed as trademarks. All brand names and product names used in this book and on its cover are trade names, service marks, trademarks and registered trademarks of their respective owners. The publishers and the book are not associated with any product or vendor mentioned in this book. None of the companies referenced within the book have endorsed the book.

"The winners in today's marketplace are those who can successfully out-think, not out-muscle, the competition"

– Michel Robert, The New Strategic Thinking

Contents

Part 4

Part 5

Introduction

In today's ever-evolving and complex business environment, it is crucial for leaders and their senior leadership teams (SLT) to possess and use Critical Thinking, specifically Strategic Thinking skills, to effectively navigate challenges and drive success. With the pace of change accelerating faster than ever before, leaders must be able to assess situations and make good decisions, as well as consider long-term implications for their organisation.

Critical thinking is the process of evaluating information and ideas in a systematic, objective, and analytical manner. It involves questioning assumptions, interpreting evidence, and tapping into what an organisation's individuals think, feel and believe before arriving at a conclusion. Critical thinking is an essential skill for business leaders because it allows them to make informed decisions based on a thorough understanding of the situation. It helps leaders avoid being swayed by emotional or biased reasoning and instead focuses on evidence-based analysis and the thinking of a broad cross-section of contributors.

One example of how critical thinking is essential for business leaders is the evaluation of new products. When presented with a new product idea, leaders must be able to ask critical questions such as: What is the problem that this product solves? Who is the target market, and what is the competition like? What is the financial potential, and what are the risks and opportunities? What's the strategic fit with our other products? By using critical thinking, leaders can ensure that they are making informed decisions that are grounded in reality, not wishful thinking. After all, there is no place for hope in a business plan.

This book focuses specifically on Strategic Thinking, possibly the most important area of critical thinking. Strategic Thinking involves a long-term perspective and requires an understanding of the broader context in which the organisation operates. Strategic Thinking is vital for business leaders because it helps them anticipate changes in the market and outpace the competition.

One example of how Strategic Thinking is essential for business leaders is when developing a business plan. By using Strategic Thinking, leaders can assess the organisation's strengths, weaknesses and vulnerabilities, identify opportunities and threats, and develop a plan to achieve their goals. This plan should take into account the organisation's long-term vision, the resources available, and potential challenges that may arise. By using Strategic Thinking, leaders can ensure that their business plan is robust and able to withstand changes in the market. However, it is extremely important that the Strategic Thinking is structured and carried out in the correct sequence looking through the correct lens at the correct time. This book will share the astonishingly simple recipe to deliver outstanding Strategic Thinking to sustainably grow any organisation that follows this process.

Before we get into Pies or Pie Charts it's important to clarify the difference between Strategic Thinking and strategic planning. These two terms are often used interchangeably, but they are very different. The essence of Strategic Thinking has been explained earlier. Strategic planning is the process of developing a roadmap to achieve your Strategic Thinking. In other words, once you've done the Strategic Thinking and have your goals, critical issues and deliverables are identified. You then need a strategic plan to make it all happen.

If you want a quick litmus test to see if your organisation is deploying Strategic Thinking effectively, try answering the following questions honestly:

- Is your senior leadership team (SLT) "bought into" and aligned with your growth strategy?
- Do you have an effective growth strategy that you're totally happy with?
- Does your SLT all share the same vision for the organisation?
- Can your SLT and fellow Board members each give an accurate and concise description of your growth strategy?
- How do you know? When and how did you last check?
- Do you have a mechanism to filter and allocate resources clearly and effectively?
- How do you prevent resources from being allocated to strategically misaligned activities?
- How do you identify and focus on the few opportunities or issues that will significantly move your business ahead?
- When you have a few strategic options, how do you decide which road to take?
- Do you have a genuine "game-changing" strategy?
- Do you control your market segment or do you play to rules others have set?
- Do you ever feel that you, the SLT and the business are a little cosy and comfortable?

When Strategic Thinking is missing at the top, organisations drift. Without clear direction, teams waste time on short-term fixes, opportunities slip through the cracks, and resources are spread too thin or utilised ineffectively. Momentum stalls, morale dips, and competitors pull ahead. Ultimately, the business becomes reactive rather than proactive–always busy, rarely effective, and constantly playing catch-up. In short, your competitors who are deploying Strategic Thinking will outthink, outpace and outmanoeuvre you and your business.

The book has been divided into five parts.

Part 1 – I expand further on why Strategic Thinking is important, hopefully dispelling the myth that it's difficult. explore what bad Strategic Thinking and planning can lead to. I dig a little deeper into the what, why and how of critical thinking. Finally, I explain why it's important to involve the wider leadership team.

Part 2 – I walk you through the first critical steps of the Strategic Thinking process. You'll learn how to assess your current business model, your current trading environment and how to assess your unique stakeholder landscape. You will learn how to conduct a wide and deep review of your present and future competition. I systematically take you through how to predict the changes to your future business arena. Then finally, I end where most others try to start with a SWOT analysis. However, you'll learn how to conduct a SWOT analysis properly.99% of businesses and business coaches do it wrong.

Part 3 – By this stage in the process organisations have collective clarity on where they are and what the future business arena is likely to look like. In part 3 I explore precisely how your organisation will compete and what it is going to look like. Every organisation has a driving force, but most leadership teams don't know what theirs is. I explain why it's such a powerful discovery and how to leverage it to develop a game-changing Future Strategic Profile (FSP) for your business.

Part 4 – Once you and the team have complete alignment on what you want your organisation to look like in the near future, how are you going to get there? I explain the 3 different lenses you and the SLT need to look through in order to make sure your thinking is as wide and deep as possible. Then I share how you should structure all of your incredible outputs in order to nail the critical path to take.

Part 5 – Some final thoughts and additional slices to help you on your way.

One last thing before we get started.

So why the title "Pies or Pie Charts"

At the very core of what I believe to be the most fundamental fact when it comes to Strategic Thinking and effectively executing a winning strategy is – WHO IS INVOLVED. Too many times I've seen Senior Leadership Teams (SLT) come together to review spreadsheets and pie charts produced in isolation by each functional head. After a few hours of debate and defence a compromise vanilla strategy is agreed. The very best the SLT can hope for is incremental growth. Nothing transformational can be achieved this way.

Worse still is when the CEO or Board send for some overpaid firm of consultants to produce a load of pie charts recommending a strategic direction. It might work, it might not, but if it does fail (and it probably will) we can blame the consultant, vow never to use them again and go find another firm of consultants.

At the heart of strategy and execution has to be – WHO YOU INVOLVE. Imagine your SLT for a moment is a huge tray of perfectly baked pies. From the outside they all look pretty similar. Until you sample the pies, slice them open so to speak, you have no idea what's inside. You have no idea what different flavours they have inside. Your SLT, and in fact, all your people have so much treasure inside. This wealth of experience, know-how, perspective and creativity is hidden in plain sight. Developing your strategy for your business is exactly the same. You have to find out and harness what your SLT and key people "think, feel and believe". The best chance of success is a strategy developed by the entire SLT plus other key people who are deemed to be your next wave of talent. Not only will it be far richer, but, because they designed it, they'll be totally committed to seeing it through.

So that's it – Pies or Pie Charts. Truly harness your key people or stick to functional silo thinking and the annual planning game?

So that's it, let's crack on with learning how to think strategically.

Scan the QR code for the video:
Why is this book important?

Part 1

Why is Strategic Thinking important, yet so rarely deployed?

The Nine Danger Signals

The Strategic Thinking frame outlined later in this book has been used by myself and other DPI partners in well over 3500 businesses since Mike Robert kicked everything off in the early 1980s. That's over 3500 businesses that recognised they could do better at critical thinking. If I look back at my own experiences prior to using DPI in Europe, I can recall feeling that there had to be a better way. The way we did our annual strategic plan felt very clunky, disconnected and regimented. We were following a planning timeline driven by the Finance Director.

Scan the QR code for this chapter's video

Fast forward to 2013. It wasn't difficult to pinpoint a few warning signals that we could advise clients to watch out for; some were obvious, yet very smart leadership teams still do it, time after time. If only I could push the pause button and really nail the danger signals leaders should watch out for. Then it would be kind of self-selecting, they'd be able to scorecard their own situation and bring in help if one or more of the signs were evident in the way they developed the strategy for their business.

Then, in spring of 2015 another DPI partner Nigel Cork and I were heading back from a brilliant but exhausting Strategic Thinking workshop in some remote corner of Switzerland. It was literally planes, trains and automobiles to get there and back. We had a couple of hours to kill while waiting for our flight back to the UK. We went through our collective experiences and came up with nine warning signs or danger signals to watch out for if you're a CEO or on a leadership team. If any of these are familiar to you, then you need to rethink how you go about formulating your strategy.

But what should we call this new filter we'd developed? We came up with "The Nine Danger Signals of Strategy". I did say we were both tired.

9	DANGER SIGNALS SCORECARD	SCORE
1	BUDGETING PROCESS IS DULL	
2	COMPETITOR OBSESSIVE COMPULSIVE DISORDER (C.O.C.D) IS PRESENT	
3	CORNER OFFICE SYNDROME	
4	TOO MANY OPPORTUNITIES	
5	TOO MUCH POWERPOINT	
6	ELEVATOR PITCH FAIL	
7	NUMBER CRUNCHITIS	
8	GOOD IDEAS, POOR EXECUTION	
9	THE IMPLICIT STRATEGY	
	TOTAL	

Figure 1.3

The Nine Danger Signals of Strategy

If you're anything like me, you love simple, easy-to-follow self-assessment tools. Well, that's how you should use the 9 Danger Signals. Be brutally honest and assess which of the following exist in your business today:

1. The Budgeting Process is Dull

There are companies in the world whose CEOs care more about the venue and the menu than about unlocking proper wide and deep Strategic Thinking amongst their leadership team. They think more about the hotel in which to hold the retreat and the restaurant they'll be going to for dinner than the process they'll deploy. Rather than: What's really going on right now, what's around the corner and where our business should be heading.

Those CEOs are probably buried in the mire brought about by the first Strategy Danger Signal: The Budgeting Process is Dull.

Of all the danger signals and mistakes that can be made in formulating a growth strategy, this is probably the biggest and most common one out of all of them.

That's the beauty of danger *signals* – they point to an underlying problem that is not yet perhaps entirely visible.

Too often, a company does not have any transversal thinking, no collective joined-up thinking between key functions, no critical thinking, nothing. What they have is, in fact, an "Annual Planning Cycle".

An All-Too-Common Scenario – The Financial Director and "The Budget"

Here's a typical scenario that I have experienced and observed in 90% of the companies we've been invited to help.

That Annual Planning Cycle is often driven by Finance. So, the Finance Director or CFO will sidle up to the CEO and say, "Okay, boss, it's that time of year again. What I'll do is I'll send out the spreadsheets and I'll ask each function to prepare a presentation and put the numbers in there…" and so … the Planning Game begins.

So, for functions such as Sales, Marketing, HR & training and IT etc, they'll create their action plans for the coming year and enter all their numbers into the spreadsheet. This could be for building a new service or building a new website, training customer service staff on how to do XYZ, etc. They know that the unwritten rule of the Planning Game is to inflate what you really need by circa 20% or, if you are Sales, reduce the target you believe you can actually achieve by, say, 10%. Then everybody vies to win the "powerpoint challenge". This is a critical part of the Planning Game. Distract the audience, specifically the CEO and CFO/FD, sufficiently away from the numbers with a powerpoint masterclass of promise upon promise of awesomeness.

Whilst rarely successful, it doesn't stop them trying.

However, the week before the strategy day, the CEO calls up the CFO/FD and says while looking at the spreadsheet, "Okay, FD. What do the numbers look like?" The FD says, "Well, we wanted 10% growth in both revenue and EBIT. According to these numbers, we're only going to get 5% and 3% growth. The CFO/FD then makes personal recommendations on where costs can be removed and sales targets increased.

The FD or CEO will drive the timeline and the process. They book a hotel somewhere, get everyone together to show their presentations and talk about their numbers. (Or maybe they'll just go into the boardroom.)

So here's the fun part. The CEO and CFO/FD know all about the planning game and the powerpoint challenge. They played it themselves for many years. Now the poachers have turned into gamekeepers. They only really want or expect a 10% increase in Sales, but…. "Okay, we need you to increase Sales by 18.5%". The Sales Director launches into their well-rehearsed mitigation arguments etc. The rest of the room goes into a cold sweat because they know what's coming. They're next….

The Marketing Director does the same, but on the opposite tack: They ask for double the budget to execute all these elaborate digital and social campaigns, knowing they're going to have that budget cut. Next UP…. IT and so on.

FAILING FAST
ISN'T ENOUGH
-WIN FAST.
AMPLIFY
SUCCESS AND
SCALE WHAT
WORKS!

Another more subtle aspect to the Dull Budgeting Process is the "you leave me alone and I'll leave you alone". Each functional head knows that if they throw hand grenades they'll get them thrown back. If the mud-slinging begins then "Inter-departmental warfare" will ensue.

The game of cat and mouse is over, finally. The Pie charts are finalised, numbers agreed and they all head off to the Restaurant licking their wounds but relieved that the whole charade is over for another year.

This repetitive dull planning game is played out in many boardrooms across the world. I see it everywhere. The real tragedy is that the leadership team often thinks they are being rigorous and challenging. Tell me, where is the Strategic Thinking? We might see pockets of it within the odd function, we might even see neighbour functions like Marketing and Sales collaborate a little. The epic tragedy is that we will only ever see incremental improvement at best. To unlock the true potential of the leadership team and the business, they'll have to find another way.

Put Strategic Thinking first, get the whole team working on it together and get their buy in. Then work on the plan and budget.

2. COCD – Competitor Obsessive-Compulsive Disorder

If you spend too much time focusing on *one single competitor* or a *single group of competitors* you could develop tunnel vision and completely miss the new player who has just entered your sandbox (extended marketplace) and suddenly steals the whole game from you.

This is what I've termed COCD – Competitor Obsessive-Compulsive Disorder.

Whilst not a recognised medical condition, trust me, it's very real.

UK Supermarkets Suffered from COCD

A great example of COCD is the big five supermarkets in the UK. (I must remind you that I am speaking as a professional outsider looking in – I have never worked with the names I'm about to mention, but as an observer and an experienced consultant with big firms, I've put this theory together of what happened to them when two new players entered the arena.)

Asda, Tesco, Sainsbury's, Morrisons and Waitrose were *so focused on each other* and in competing with one another, that they completely missed the entrance of Aldi and Lidl who came into the fray like dark knights from the proverbial fog. They were small fry, thought the Big Five, and had no chance in the UK marketplace.

Aldi and Lidl completely revolutionised the way supermarkets in the UK could operate. They challenged and changed some of the core fundamental beliefs and practices that had stood for decades.

While the 5 big chains were all busy trying to outdo each other in terms of pricing, and Waitrose was busy reinforcing its premium position against M&S, Aldi and Lidl were thinking "outside the box" and came in with a completely different business model and customer-focused offer. They were not only cheaper, but smarter too.

All of the UK supermarket chains' advertising was entirely obsessed with their competitors. "Our average shopping basket size is £20 cheaper than Tesco!" or "We've just launched a new Value range which is now cheaper than Sainsbury's!"

The name of the game for these five players was to have the *broadest* range of products possible so that you could have the *maximum* choice at the best price. And we had these great big, huge supermarkets getting bigger and bigger.

And, suddenly, Lidl and Aldi came in and said, "Right, instead of three hundred thousand SKUs or items, we're going to have fifteen hundred. We'll have all the essentials. We're not going to have twelve different types of chocolate digestive biscuits. We'll have *one*. And we'll have *one* passata sauce and *one* ketchup".

"We'll also run some of our own-brand stuff where the quality is good, but because we're very simple, and our supply chain is simple, we'll be able to be very competitive on price".

"The store designs are going to be very different. Basically, we're only going to have three aisles, and they're going to be very long. And that middle aisle will become legendary for those wacky, crazy things that always change from month to month. And we'll make a big deal out of this. We'll even change the way our customers bag their purchases at check out to speed up the throughput by 50%".

"So, in March, just before the fishing season starts, we'll have loads of fishing stuff – waders and fishing rods and bait. Then, in April, it's barbecue season so we'll have all the barbecue attachments and gizmos and stuff you might need for your barbecue, or outdoor gardening."

Aldi and Lidl *completely* rethought the model and outdid the competition.

Now, everything you see at Aldi is available at Sainsbury's or one of the other big chains. It's somewhere there.

But Sainsbury's and the other big stores have a supply chain geared for 300,000 products, while Aldi has one geared for 1,500. You end up paying 30% less for your shopping at Aldi and Lidl, with little or no compromise on quality.

Their market share, today, continues to grow. Kantar reported their combined market share as 12% on 3 December 2017, already more than Morrison's share of 10.6%. On 9th August 2020 their combined market share was 13.8% and was as high as 14.1% in December of the previous year. The Guardian reported in January 2020 that Aldi had a staggering 874 stores in the UK and was planning on having 1025 by 2025.

The numbers are simply astronomical, their growth strategy phenomenal.

Aldi and Lidl changed the game, and the other players were caught flat-footed. They had COCD.

Every Industry Suffers from This

Every industry probably has a couple of these lead players looking at each other from over the fence.

And, suddenly, Player Number Five (in terms of Market Share) comes along, does some proper Strategic Thinking that leads to a bit of innovation which drives its market share up dramatically because the big players are far too busy watching each other – they're all suffering from COCD.

Another problem with COCD is that you end up letting your competitors determine what actions you take and which strategies you implement. You end up letting *them* dictate what you should be doing.

As a business, if you find yourself *fixated* on your primary competitor; if you find that your meetings spend an inordinate amount of time discussing that competitor, you could be suffering from COCD.

And, be forewarned, excessive fixation on one or two or three *main* competitors will leave you blind to the player who comes in from the north or south and completely changes the game.

We need to remove these links.

3. Corner Office Syndrome

Corner Office Syndrome occurs when every departmental head has to come over to the CEO's office to share their ideas.

I've seen this happen many times. And the two main reasons it happens are because:

1. The CEO is a "Big Personality", almost like a "Superstar" in the employees' minds.
2. The CEO is a tyrant, instilling the fear of God into their employees.

Let's look at each one of these.

The Big Personality CEO

Great, your employees think you're a superstar. Yay! Or *is* it great?

Some people have magnetic, charismatic personalities and a lot of successful CEOs are this way. When you think of Elon Musk, or of someone like Dan Price who took a massive pay cut to ensure his employees could earn a better wage, you immediately get the impression that these people are massive personalities.

A boss who is a big personality in a positive sense and a great leader can unwittingly bring about Corner Office Syndrome in the business.

This can lead to people rushing up to the CEO's office, overeager to please, and saying, "Hey, boss, check out what I've done today!" for every single idea.

Everybody wants to show off to them or impress them or bring everything to them and delight them as the head of the company.

This syndrome can prevent people from making decisions, they're constantly looking for affirmation. Like an enthusiastic bunch of puppies they're looking to get stroked by the boss. What will they do if the CEO is away for a month?

The Tyrannical Megalomaniac

And then there's the Corner Office Syndrome brought about by the tyrant and megalomaniac. Or the Control Freak.

In this case, people are terrified of the boss and feel they have to bring their ideas to them just so they aren't shot down in flames, publicly, later in the Boardroom. They're made insecure by the boss's presence and feel uncertain about their future.

Any independent thinkers will undoubtedly leave to work elsewhere. What you are left with is a bunch of terrified toothless executives paid a lot of money to agree with everything the boss says. Their entire modus operandi is survival, keeping their heads down. They often manage upwards, pleasing the boss and ensuring that if things go wrong, they are good at shifting any blame onto their team or, better still, other departments.

The results are the same, albeit for a different reason: Corner Office Syndrome.

The first personality type – the positive Big Personality – is much more subtle to observe when it comes to Corner Office Syndrome. The tyrant is easier to spot.

This style of management is very "last-century", but, sadly, still very present in this one.

The Filter – the "Codir"

Paul-Marie Chavanne was President of the DPD Group when I served as the group's CMO between 2005-2012 in Paris.

He was also the best boss I've ever had.

Paul-Marie was the one who convinced me to move to Paris. One of my few regrets is that I never mastered the French language (I didn't even come close), but he never held it against me. Although, I'm certain it disappointed him.

Unfortunately, this affability of his resulted in a company culture of everybody always going to him to tell him their idea. Everybody wanted to please him.

What he did to resolve this was create something which he termed the *codir*, short for "*comité direction*".

Basically, the *Codir* was a meeting of his direct reports. Every Monday morning, from 8:30 to 9:30, all his direct reports would gather in the Boardroom and each would have max five mins to update him and the rest of the room on what they were focusing on. This gave them a window to ask his opinion or advice.

It was genius, his *Codir* then stopped everybody running to him every hour to bring their insights, challenges, opinions and project updates to him. Your issue needed to be pretty significant to justify a separate interruption or meeting. It allowed him to listen and choose the stuff he wanted to hear more about. He could then manage his week with minimal interruptions.

To this day, the *Codir* is the best treatment for Corner Office Syndrome I have ever come across.

I talk a little more about filters later on.

4. Too Many Opportunities

Imagine taking a busload of children to a toy store. (And if you're not a parent and cannot correctly envisage that scenario, let me summarise in four words: *Total mayhem and anarchy*.)

"Too Many Opportunities" is like that, but in a business context. Everyone has a ton of ideas and they're running off chasing all the new shiny toys.

But there's no real focus.

This is "Too Many Opportunities", and it can negatively impact your ability to clearly focus on your strategy.

Things become overly fragmented and, before you know it, the business is all over the place.

We've all been there – we've all worked with colleagues who come into the office in the morning with some fresh idea that's "going to be brilliant!"

Innovation is great, in fact, it's essential. Ideas are an important part of any innovation, the first domino so to speak.

But before that idea can take root in any way, it must pass through a filter.

I talk quite a bit more in this book about Filters, so that you can have a good idea of it and use it in your strategies.

Essentially, to get stuff done you need a clear aligned direction and clear goals and strategies to get you there. Ideas that don't contribute directly should be seen as noise and cancelled out.

5. Too Much PowerPoint

When someone lacks substance for their recommendation, they often cover it up with a fancy PowerPoint presentation. Okay, reading that back, it sounds a bit harsh. But, honestly, it's often true. How many times have you seen fancy PowerPoint decks with shed loads of graphics and pie charts? With the emergence of AI making it easier than ever to produce great slides, searching for the true value within is only set to become even harder.

If this is becoming the norm in your business, watch out!

Ever heard the saying: "Death by PowerPoint"?

A guy who worked for me in Paris, let's just call him JC, was a classic example of this. He was very bright and had worked in consultancy for years. I think this was only his second role "client side". He'd picked up a lot of bad habits from consulting.

And he was an absolute *master* at creating really fancy PowerPoint slides, bold visuals, bold messages and even bolder claims.

When you strip it all down, there's often very little relevance or substance behind it.

The big consulting firms are brilliant at this, painting this illusion of awesomeness. Hogging way too much of the meeting time on slick presentations. Seducing the audience into feeling what they want you to feel.

Try telling them to close the laptop lid and talk me through it. Chuck them a pen and flip chart if it helps. Wipe the gloss off the messaging and get to the heart of the proposition. Essentially, be in a position where the content can be judged purely on its merits and nothing else.

6. Elevator Pitch

One of the most critical factors in any successful business has to be the degree of alignment amongst leaders, middle leaders and the rest of the team. In other words, within these groups, are all parties aligned and in full agreement on what the critical issues are? What should be our direction of travel?

Another critical factor for any successful business is the degree of alignment between the layers and verticals of your organisation. By verticals, I mean the functions, regions etc. If you have a massive spread of opinion amongst your employees, or between them and the leadership team, then without doubt something is wrong and you have a problem.

The good news is that this is relatively easy to spot and resolve.

Imagine you're in a thirty-second elevator ride with your biggest customer or most significant investor. Could you summarise in those thirty seconds;

- What's great about your business? Or
- What are the key focus areas for growth for the coming 3 years? Or
- What is our purpose and values? Or
- What are our 4 biggest challenges this year?

You get the picture, identify some key *testing questions.* Answer them yourself. Hopefully that wasn't too difficult. If it was and you really had to think about it, don't worry, you're reading the right book.

However, importantly, how would your leadership team answer these questions? What about your middle leaders? Or wider staff?

Having an *effective strategy* is of course critical. But having everybody aligned behind the *effective strategy* is equally as important. The Strategy Alignment Grid illustrates very simplistically where you and your business need to be aiming for. The top right hand corner, where you have an effective strategy which is well understood throughout the organisation.

So, identify the critical questions that will flush out whether your strategy is effective and then select key individuals at all levels and ask them the questions. Score their responses and plot them on the grid below. In this example 10 is absolute optimum and 1 is shockingly poor.

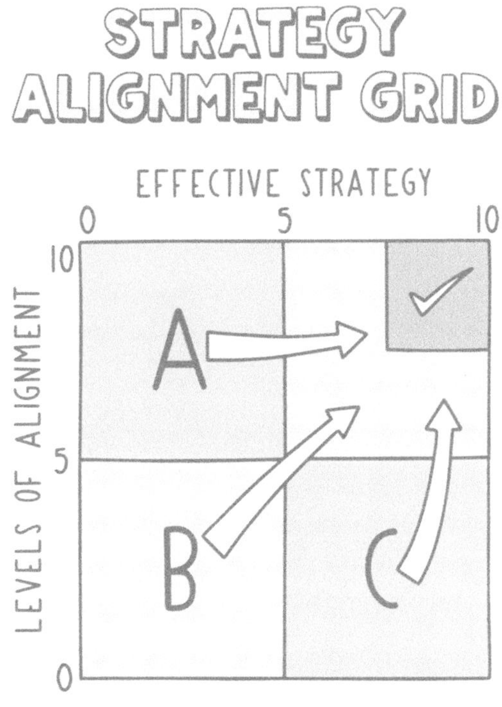

Figure 1.3.1

If they're clustered in "A" then they're reasonably aligned but behind an inadequate or unconvincing strategy. If they're in "C" you believe that the strategy in your head is good and will deliver results, but nobody else or few are behind it. This strategy was probably created by an elite few, or perhaps just you? If the responses are in the "B" area then you're screwed.

7. Number Crunchitis

Number Crunchitis is when the business is continuously looking at, say, last quarter's results, or year-on-year figures, or how the previous six months' sales numbers look against the plan. For sure, it is important to track progress and momentum. "If you measure it you can manage it". But... critically, make sure you fence off some time to look ahead and beyond.

"Spend min. 50% of your time looking to the future."

There's absolutely a time and place for reviewing the numbers. But it's imperative that your regular SLT meetings (usually once a month) dedicate at least 50% of their time and attention to the future.

Take a look at the last few SLT meetings, be honest, create a simple Pie Chart apportioning time spent reviewing the past, the current and designing the future. I choose the word designing deliberately. Looking at the financial projection or head count projected numbers doesn't count. These are most likely extrapolations of the historic and current numbers. What I mean by "designing the future" is exactly that. It's the time you spend in your regular SLT meetings to think and shape future change in your organisation.

During that 50% agenda time the team should look at and discuss opportunities and what *might* happen, not what has already happened.

A large cause of this is what we discussed in the "Budgeting Process is Dull" section, driven by a Finance Director who puts budgets up and demands to know why you're 2%overspent or under achieving ...

If you only look backwards, you'll only make incremental steps. Exploring possibilities in the future will lead to better questions, better thinking, better decision-making and of course, better progress.

8. Good Ideas, Poor Execution

There are many, many papers and books written around the subject of Great Strategy – poorly executed. The common consensus seems to be that to be successful, it's about 10% great strategy and 90% focus on great execution. Strategy should be all about quality thinking and execution is all about quality of the execution plan. As Benjamin Franklin said, "fail to plan, plan to fail".

A personal favourite anecdotal story is about the Vauxhall Nova. A sporty hatchback from the GM motor company stable that was very popular in the late 80's early 90's. It was a nippy, reliable car, perfect for running around cities. The problem came when they launched it in Spanish speaking countries. "Nova" in Spanish means "not going" or "no go" or "slow" or "not working". It meant Opel, the brand name GM used in Continental Europe, had to unpick everything and choose a new name for the car.

That's terrible execution. It hadn't been thought through properly.

But bad execution can also come about as a result of not implementing the seven elements of the Growth Grid (see last section of this book) such as:

- Not resourcing properly
- Not having the right skills

- Not incentivising your people
- Not getting a *clear* action plan in place
- Not getting the Senior Management Team to buy into the project
- And so on.

I see this Danger Signal *a lot* in the companies I deal with. The problem is also often due to a lack of management commitment or the absence of a clear plan. It can often boil down to lack of clarity, lack of focus, and the absence of sufficient capability or capacity.

Essentially, leaders need to deploy a complete and effective programme management solution across the organisation to ensure effective execution of their strategy.

9. The Implicit Strategy

The strategy is implicit – at least it is to the CEO. But nobody else really knows it, and they keep needing to come to the boss to check if their ideas are acceptable, because nobody's exactly clear about the focus or priorities in the CEO's head.

Another useful term for this is "Strategy by Osmosis" or "Leadership by Osmosis".

It often occurs when the leader is an "Ideas Person" but not an excellent communicator of those ideas. As a result, the team is left somewhat in the dark about the strategy. Equally, it can be caused because the leader generates fresh ideas frequently. The team has just gotten used to one direction when they realise the CEO has changed direction and is heading somewhere else. Or their priorities have shifted significantly.

The team *thinks* they understand the strategy, but, in fact they are now out of step with the CEO.

A leader needs to ensure that everyone is entirely clear on the strategy as well as what their goals are in trying to get there.

I frequently see the following: the boss, or another leadership team member, spends some time with a manager or employee. They start discussing: *What's going on? What are the issues? What do they need?* etc. Before you know it, there's a memo going out changing some fundamental process all on the say-so of one 15 minute conversation. A leader must robustly evaluate the messages they receive from individuals and evaluate carefully the full impact of taking the recommended decision or action.

Equally, they must be careful with the "words of wisdom" that they impart to their staff. Words of encouragement or praise can be rapidly distorted by individuals in order to get a pet project re-prioritised or get their private agenda endorsed. I've lost count of the number of times functional heads "name bomb" to give better weight behind their initiative, opinion or project. When I worked in DPD's HQ in Paris I used to wish I had a € for every time I heard functional heads name-drop Paul-Marie Chavanne in order to get ahead or get their project given the red carpet treatment.

The Weekly Reset Button

I address the Reset Button in more depth a little later in the book, but here's a quick overview.

One way to minimise this effect is to push a Weekly Reset Button and get everyone back on track regarding the current priorities.

Get everyone together, push that button and announce, "Okay, guys, don't forget: Our main priority at the moment is to do *this, this and this.*"

This keeps everybody on the same page, keeps the team focused, and prevents them from being steered off course by every little comment from the CEO or their manager or anyone else in authority.

Fig 1.3 is the 9 Danger signals scorecard. Give it a go by giving your organisation a score out of 10 for each issue. Let's assume a high score means that you believe that danger signal is a significant problem.

	9 DANGER SIGNALS SCORE CARD	SCORE
1	BUDGETING PROCESS IS DULL	
2	COMPETITOR OBSESSIVE COMPULSIVE DISORDER (C.O.C.D) IS PRESENT	
3	CORNER OFFICE SYNDROME	
4	TOO MANY OPPORTUNITIES	
5	TOO MUCH POWERPOINT	
6	ELEVATOR PITCH FAIL	
7	NUMBER CRUNCHITIS	
8	GOOD IDEAS. POOR EXECUTION	
9	THE IMPLICIT STRATEGY	
	TOTAL	

Figure 1.3

Key Takeaways

Dull planning processes can lead to interdepartmental warfare, petty "planning games" and general disgruntlement. Avoid this by establishing a *Strategic Thinking* process which in turn will create a strong plan and drive it. Adopt this new approach and dump the planning cycle that has been stifling the thinking.

Competitor Obsessive Compulsive Disorder can result in the SLT wearing blinkers. They become blind to new players who might change the game entirely and catch your company flat-footed.

Corner Office Syndrome can happen because of a magnetic personality or a tyrant. Instigate a short punchy *Codir* which gives every director access to you regularly so they don't need to constantly seek one-on-one time.

Too many opportunities can lead to mayhem. Again, in this case, a filtering process is your friend. If it doesn't pass through the filter and it's not on the runway – stop it in its tracks.

Too much PowerPoint occurs when ideas lack substance. Ask for substance, and try not to be fooled by glossy presentations.

Regularly test your people with a key question but limit their response to 30 seconds.

Number Crunchitis ensues when the team is too focused on the past. Be sure to spend at least 50% of your SLT meetings discussing opportunities and *the future* in order to make those *Big Steps* required for company growth.

Poor execution – check out the Growth Grid. Essentially, deploy an effective programme management system. Make sure everybody uses a consistent and simple project management system.

The Implicit Strategy results in staff being thrown off course by every little comment made by the CEO. Communicate your strategy clearly, and do it *weekly* by pushing a Reset Button which gets everyone on the same page.

Get Started

1. Get your team together and ask them some **killer questions** about your business. Get them to *write down the answers* without discussing them, or perhaps video each person giving an answer in a private room. Then compare the answers. Plot them on the Strategy Alignment Grid.

2. Take each of the 9 Danger Signals (see fig 1.3) and give your organisation a score out of 10 for each. Involve some or all of your SLT as well. If you score higher than five for any of them, start to prioritise and put an action plan together.

3. Think about whether your business could start to hold some sort of weekly "stand-up" or Codir?

BETTER
QUESTIONS
=
BETTER
THINKING
=
BETTER
OUTCOMES

Growing Too Fast – Push That Reset Button

Business commentators often cite Premature Scaling as the number one reason for start-up failure.

Scan the QR code for this chapter's video

Put simply, Premature Scaling means "growing too fast" or "too much happening, too soon".

But how can "growing fast" be an issue? Surely the purpose of any business is to *grow*?

Many of the more vocal coaches out there will have a briefcase or a laptop filled with motivational soundbites and bold "WOW claims". "30X growth in 30 months". Beware!!! Unless you've got the perfect blend of unique product, instant massive scaling capability, no or weak competition and suddenly everybody needs what you're selling. Then it's almost certainly total bullshit.

Growing faster than you and/or your people can think, or faster than your processes can cope is a significant issue in business.

Warning Symptoms That You're Growing Too Fast

If all – or a significant few – of the following warning symptoms exist in your business, you need to push the Reset Button.

"Pushing the Reset Button" means you have to pause and regroup, then go again. At the end of this section, I'll give you some tips on how to do just that.

This is not a complete list, but these are the most common I've seen over the last 20 years or so.

The following symptoms indicate an underlying organisational sickness, and the only cure is to regroup, do some Strategic Thinking, put the necessary processes in place, and get a plan in place– in short: push the Reset Button.

List of Warning Symptoms

- If you start compromising on the quality and "fit" of people you're bringing into your business, that's a warning signal that you're growing too fast. Poor hires can be hugely expensive and potentially cost you your business.

- A different shade of this symptom is that you do bring in the right people, but they don't get onboarded properly, they're sent to the front lines too soon. This damages the customer experience. Your new hire turnover is unacceptably high….
- As a result of this, the culture or DNA that you loved about your business ends up being compromised, diluted or lost. You don't recognise the business anymore. That buzz, spirit or spark just isn't what it was.
- Your people have morphed into workaholics. Many are consistently working long hours, but not on exciting new game-changing stuff, they're putting out fires and papering over the cracks.
- The buzz you used to have for your business and operations is gone. And, you're not alone, many other colleagues feel the same way.
- Your people simply can't absorb any more. They're overwhelmed. The number of your people taking sick days or having stress related issues is increasing significantly.
- Operations are struggling to deliver the proposition. Whether it's products or a service, the reliability and consistency is not what you or your customers demand.
- Often, as a result of your sales team starting to overpromise, they talk up the proposition as they chase ever increasing targets. They know it's all built on sand. Your better sales people are leaving.
- There's too much focus on the future and not enough time and energy placed on delivering an *extraordinary* customer experience *today*. It's all about balance, looking forward should represent about 50% of the SLT's time. However, don't be obsessive about it, try to get the balance right.
- Customer complaints increase dramatically and become louder. This is an inevitable symptom of poor CX (customer experience) and over-promising sales. But, the reason this is listed separately is that this is very visible and measurable.
- Customer service becomes shoddy and simple tasks fall through the cracks. This could be because of one or all of the following: under resourcing, inadequate training, poor levels of engagement, poor customer service processes.
- Because your systems and services can't cope with the demand, your products and services end up being compromised.
- Your IT runway is getting longer and wider. Then take a closer look. If the width and length is driven by "fix" projects rather than new innovation projects this usually indicates that you're constantly putting a "band-aid" on the problem but not fundamentally resolving it.
- Your training and development budget has progressively reduced. Your people and your managers simply do not have the time to identify and invest in the training and development they need to evolve and progress appropriately.

- Your SLT meetings are focussed almost entirely on operational and IT issues and discussions. Entire agendas are consumed by problem resolution when these meetings should be focused on the customer and the future.

Finally, your **purpose** and **values** are lost in the fog of expansion and bottom-line obsession.

To keep it super simple, I've made the "*growing pain pulse*" binary. Simply answer yes or no to the 15 statements below;

	THE GROWING PAIN PULSE	YES/NO
1	DECLINE IN QUALITY OF OUR PEOPLE	
2	ONBOARDING PROCESS CAN'T COPE	
3	CULTURE COMPROMISE	
4	OUR PEOPLE WORKING LONG HOURS	
5	OUR BUZZ IS FLAT	
6	SICKNESS DAYS INCREASING	
7	PRODUCT/SERVICE RELIABILITY DROPPING	
8	SALES ARE OVER PROMISING TO CLIENTS	
9	TOO MUCH FOCUS ON FUTURE	
10	CUSTOMER COMPLAINTS INCREASING	
11	SHODDY CUSTOMER SERVICE	
12	SIGNIFICANT IT FOCUS ON FIXING ISSUES	
13	TRAINING & DEVELOPMENT SPEND REDUCING	
14	SLT MEETINGS CONSUMED BY PROBLEMS	
15	OUR PURPOSE & VALUES ARE IGNORED	

Fig 1.4.1c

What to do if you're growing too fast?

I would suggest that if you have answered "yes" to more than three of the above 15 indicators, you may have a problem. As I mentioned, the above list is far from comprehensive. But if you spot a majority or *significant few* of the above symptoms in your business, it's time to push the Reset Button.

How does one do that? There isn't a big red button in the middle of every office in the world which stops growth and gets everybody back on track. Also, let's be clear. It may not be appropriate to slam the sales door shut completely. It might be essential that you maintain levels of sales. What I'm advocating for here is recognising that you cannot continue without addressing the resulting issues. If these remain unchecked and are allowed to continue, your business will fail.

The Reset Button Formula

Pushing the Reset Button follows an exact formula.

1. Take a **deliberate** and **controlled** time-out with your team.
2. Use an appropriate framework and **external facilitator** to regroup and reassess.
3. **Identify** your offensive and defensive objectives.
4. Identify what needs to change with your **future business model**
5. **Identify** those quick wins that will bring a buzz and energy levels back.
6. Break your plan up into 90-day sprints and take some control back

Bring the fun and purpose back into your business. Get your "company mojo" back by taking fast action at the first signs of the symptoms above, and push that Reset Button to get things rolling again.

Key Takeaways

Premature Scaling is often cited as the number one reason that start-ups fail.

Growing faster than your people and processes can cope with is bad.

The quality of your thinking has a direct impact on the quality of your thriving.

There are many warning symptoms to indicate the underlying organisational sickness of growing too fast.

If you spot many or a significant few of these symptoms in your business, you need to push the Reset Button.

Call a time-out, and regroup. Take control back.

Get Started

1. Look over your business and compare it to the list of warning symptoms given in the *Growing Pain Pulse*
2. If your business has many or a significant few of the above warning signals, work out how you can push the Reset Button at your office, including who to use as an external facilitator, and get your team back on track.

Critical Thinking: What? Why? How?

Henry Ford once said, "Thinking is the hardest work there is, which is probably the reason so few engage in it."

I'm bordering on being obsessive about helping individuals and teams to enjoy *critical thinking* and then thrive as a direct result.

Indeed, by reading this book and applying its contents, you are engaging in an action explicitly designed to improve the way you think. If you and your team adopt the principles and practices of this book you will improve the quality of your thinking – guaranteed.

Scan the QR code for this chapter's video

Better questions = Better thinking = Better outcomes.

What is Critical Thinking?

The word "critical" has two well-known meanings in the English language.

To understand this concept, it is essential to define precisely what we mean by "critical".

Merriam-Webster Dictionary defines *critical* as[1]:

"1 a: inclined to criticise severely and unfavourably"
"1 c: exercising or involving careful judgment or judicious evaluation"

The first meaning is negative and not very helpful – ever.

When discussing Critical Thinking, we are using the second meaning above – *judicious* evaluation, which itself means an evaluation done using good judgment, taking all factors into account, involving analysis.

The Oxford English Dictionary takes this a step further and actually defines Critical Thinking as a phrase in itself:

"The objective analysis and evaluation of an issue in order to form a judgement."

An SLT that practices Critical Thinking puts the power into the business' hands to analyse and evaluate their business issues in order to form an optimum judgment.

Indeed, for the last few years at the World Economic Forum in Davos, Critical Thinking has been identified as the number one and most important skill required by business leaders.

Critical Thinking applies both at a personal and a business level.

---

[1] https://www.merriam-webster.com/dictionary/critical

Why Critical Thinking?

There have been four industrial revolutions. We are currently living through the fourth one.

Every single one of these industrial revolutions was brought about *directly* by innovators and entrepreneurs who knew how to engage in Critical Thinking.

They knew how to "analyse and evaluate an issue in order to form a judgment".

And their inventions and innovations didn't just *disrupt* a market, they changed the world to the point where that world changed utterly, and forever.

I won't bore you with an extensive history of it (I'm no historian myself), but here are some quick key points to illustrate this fact.

The First Industrial Revolution occurred in the late 18th century as a result of mechanisation, and the increased use of steam and water power.

Before the first industrial revolution, people mostly produced textiles at home.

Innovations and inventions in the field of *cast iron* production led directly to innovations and inventions in the way textiles were created. New inventions in cotton spinning completely revolutionised the way it was done, increasing output to staggering heights.

Some of the critical disruptors and innovators of this time were:

- Edmund Cartwright who designed the first power loom in 1784.
- James Hargreaves who invented the "spinning jenny" – a machine used in weaving.
- Eli Whitney who invented the cotton gin.
- Edward Somerset who invented the steam engine.

The full list is enormous.

And it's the same for each of the subsequent Industrial Revolutions.

The Second Industrial Revolution occurred in the late 19th century, and was the revolution which resulted in mass production and the advent of electricity.

This, too, was driven by critical thinkers Alexander Graham Bell and the modern telephone. Sir Henry Bessemer's invention of the first inexpensive industrial process for the mass production of steel. Harry John Lawson's invention of the bicycle and John Kemp Starley's production of the first commercially successful bicycle, resulting in a "bike boom" in the 1890s.

Critical thinkers all of them, disrupting the status quo and changing the world.

The Third Industrial Revolution has been dubbed the "Digital Revolution" and occurred in the late 20th century. Sir Timothy Berners-Lee invented the World Wide Web. The developers of specialised integrated circuits or "chips". Inventors of transistors.

Each of these inventors caused a disruption. Each was a critical thinker. Harnessing these initial breakthroughs to achieve incredible commercial or social success required Critical Thinking. An enormous list of brands like Microsoft, Apple, Meta and Tesla have SLTs that all possess one important common capability: Critical Thinking.

All of these disruptions and innovations eventually led to the Fourth Industrial Revolution we're experiencing right now: The automation of traditional manufacturing processes, the "internet of things" (everyday objects connected to the internet via sensors), smart technology, machine-to-machine communication, AI and machine learning.

Each of these significant changes was driven by an initial disruption. And that disruption was caused by a critical thinker.

The businesses and people who initiated the changes had Critical Thinking. And the businesses which thrived during these periods had Critical Thinking.

So, *why* Critical Thinking? Because you simply cannot expect to survive or to thrive without it.

Most Importantly: How to Achieve Critical Thinking

And, finally, the most essential part of this section: Exactly *how* do you achieve Critical Thinking?

The answer is both pure and simple.

To achieve critical thinking, you must ask the right questions!

Great questions equal great thinking. And flawed questions equal flawed thinking.

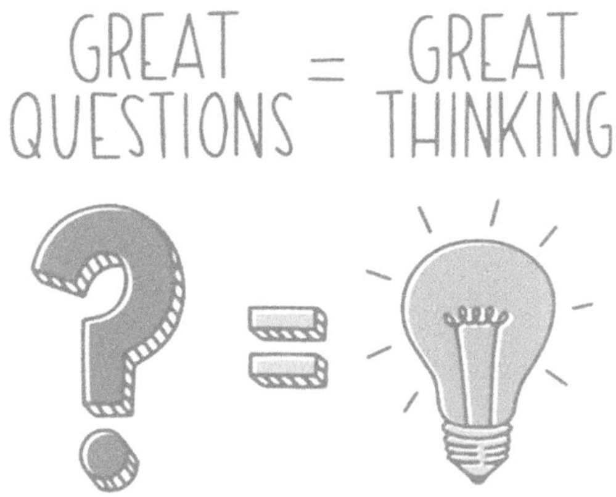

Everything we do as humans is driven by asking questions.

For instance, when waking up in the morning, a person might look out the window and ask, "Hmm, is it going to be cool later on?"

The answer to that question determines if they'll put on a fleece or jumper.

That's Critical Thinking in action at a very simplistic personal level, and it was achieved by asking the right question. If you take this logic further, you won't just take the day's weather at face value at first glance. You might look at a reliable weather app. Now we have better quality critical thinking, simply because we've taken it up a notch.

Similarly, in business decisions, the *right questions* must be asked.

"Do we need to hire ten more customer service people because we're swamped?"

That's not necessarily the right question to ask. A question that leads to critical thinking might sound more like this: "Hiring so many people is becoming labour-intensive. So, *is there a smarter way to do this?*" Or, "What can we do to our product or customer experience to reduce the proportion of customer query calls to sales ratio?" You get the idea.

To achieve critical thinking that drives your business forward, you need better-quality questions.

If you ask average questions, you will get average thinking.

The quality of the questions and the process that follows triggers the level of thinking you will achieve either individually or collectively.

Asking questions in the right order

But asking the right questions is not the only thing necessary to achieve critical thinking. You also need to ask them in the correct sequence.

This is a crucial concept that is going to come up again and again in this book. It's especially important when we talk later about what's wrong with the way companies do 'SWOT' analysis. They don't ask the right questions in the *correct sequence*, and I'll show you later on how to do just that in relation to something as simple and widely used as a SWOT analysis.

But here's a small tip: It's simply not possible to do a proper SWOT analysis of a business' strengths and weaknesses in relation to its competitors without first asking the question: "*Who* are our competitors?"

Great questions in the correct sequence equal great thinking.

Here's an "outsider looking in" example.

I've never worked with Tesla and I don't know Elon Musk.

But, as an outsider looking in, I imagine that after the phenomenal success of PayPal this entrepreneurial giant must've sat back and asked himself, "What next? What is the future of personal travel? Fossil fuels are dying out. There's an opportunity here to generate a train of enthusiasm and get everybody on board, especially major investors. To crack this, I'll need to generate *billions* of dollars in order to do the research and create the batteries, the motors …"

All of that might've begun with the right question: "*What* is the future of travel?" Or "*How* are people going to travel when fossil fuels have run out?" Or "What is the future of driving? It can't be fossil fuels. It has to be fuel cells or electric cars…"

As I said, I've never worked with or even spoken to Elon Musk, but I'd bet my last penny that he engaged in Critical Thinking by asking the *right questions* before building the empire he runs today.

Everything that is groundbreaking and new and innovative has come about because *somebody* had the vision. And they obtained that vision by *asking great questions at the right time in the right order.*

You *can* thrive in this Fourth Industrial Revolution we're in right now, but only if you ask the right quality questions that will trigger quality Critical Thinking.

Process Consulting and Critical Thinking

The most important thing in any business and for any individual is to practice the *art* of Critical Thinking and become good at it.

Acclaimed leadership and Critical Thinking expert Mike Roberts did the heavy lifting circa 40 years ago. He analysed hundreds and hundreds of businesses. Successful ones and less successful ones. He codified what made the successful business a success. He identified exactly what questions needed to be asked and in what sequence. Since then, DPI Partners and I have been the custodians of this process. We can merely claim that we've refreshed and polished those original frameworks.

When I'm invited into a business by the CEO, we galvanise the leadership team by asking the right questions in the right order and then facilitating the subsequent discussions to unlock Critical Thinking.

Thinking is nothing more than a response to a question. When we're asked to join the leadership team by orchestrating a Strategic Thinking workshop we have all the questions ready to be posed in a precise sequence. So much so that I have two giant exhibition panels that I use to dress the walls of the "war room". They measure 5m x 2.3m and 3m x 2.3m. These are used throughout the two days to explain the journey and the progress. Each poster used has its place on either "Growth Street" (5m x2.3m wall) or "Game Change Close" (3m x 2.3m wall).

Since Mike Roberts' first book on Critical Thinking some 40 years ago, several DPI partners have written their own versions. While they contain updated case studies, they haven't strayed from the process path that Mike developed all those years ago. Neither does mine to be honest. However, there is one massive difference between this book and all its predecessors' literary gems. They metaphorically showed a bit of ankle. They explained the concepts and importance behind each one. Illustrated by using many case studies where real change was seen. However, the reader would struggle to be able to do it for themselves. Clearly, that's the whole point. I have a different take on this. I believe that everybody should have a coach or a coaching solution. By extending this ethos, I believe that all should have access to the fundamental Strategic Thinking process. Therefore, this book has to go further and truly enable the reader to embark on the Strategic Thinking process themselves. We've delivered well over 3500 of these Strategic Thinking workshops globally. The IP is out there already. Sure, it's our IP, but the cat's out of the proverbial bag. When you consider that our average group size is 22, that's 77,000 people minimum who've benefited from learning the exact questions and sequence (the secret recipe). The following figure shows the entire Strategic Thinking frame.

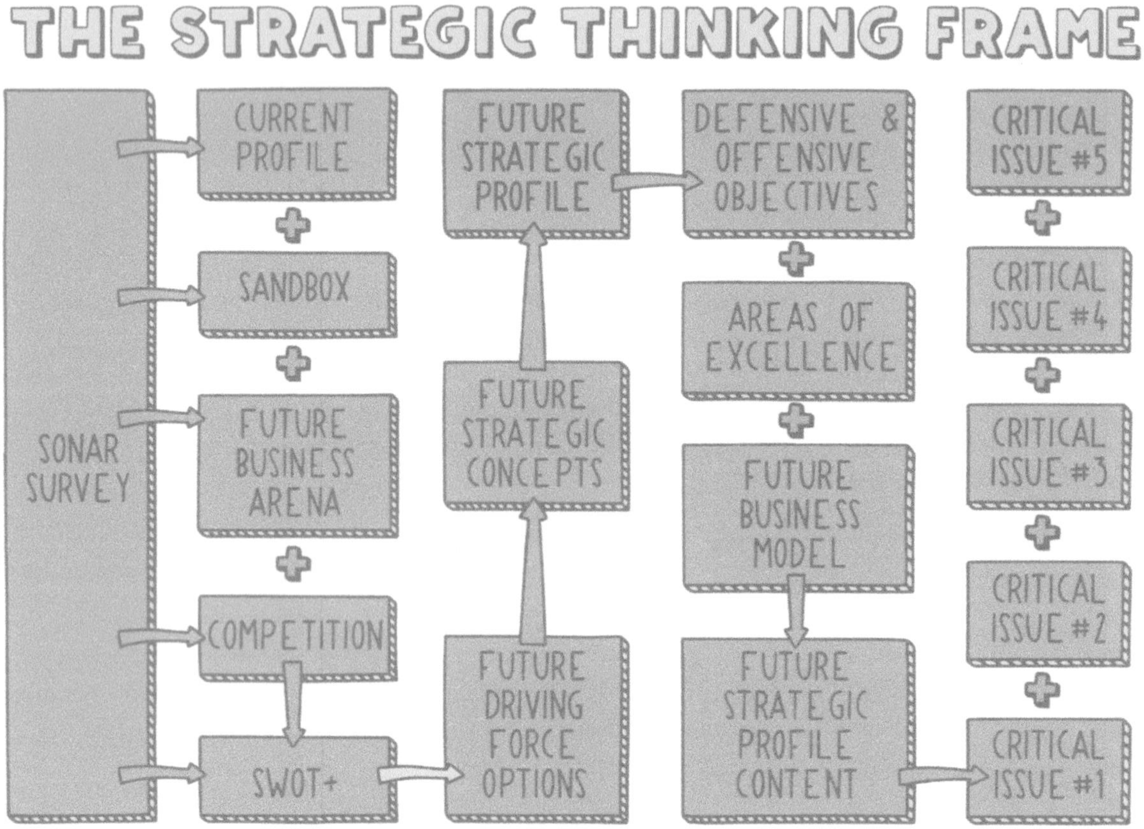

Figure 2.0c

I've gone one step further. I'm actually illustrating exactly how it's done and why. I'm passionate about driving positive change in business. That's why I co-founded peer2peer in 2017 with Simon HC, Tim Bentall and Stuart Osbourne (more about this at the end of the book). I believe you can use this book to develop your own Strategic Thinking programme with your team. Obviously, I'm hoping you'll reach out to me and the team to facilitate it for you. So, it's absolutely possible for you to DIY it. However, our facilitation and additional probing does unlock even greater insight and value. Therefore, I'm advocating for you to choose to get our team in to support you and DIP it (Do it Properly).

I have run Strategic Thinking Programmes for hundreds of clients over the last 10 years or so. Before I got involved with DPI, other practitioners around the world have delivered an estimated 3500+ Strategic Thinking programmes. What's fascinating is that in 99% of instances clients chose this framework because they were experiencing one of, or a combination of, the following:

1. The CEO or boss felt that progress was okay but could or should be better. They can't quite pinpoint exactly where the growth will come from. They practise strategic planning. Nothing's particularly wrong, everything okay, but they want way more than just okay. They want more than consistent incremental improvement. They recognised that the Strategic Thinking process is perfect if you're looking for transformational change or growth.
2. The CEO or boss can't decide which way to go. They're facing a fork in the road and the SLT is split or undecided or blissfully ignoring the situation. So, they pause and pause some more. The Strategic Thinking process is brilliant for getting rapid collective clarity on the correct direction to take.
3. The CEO or boss has just landed in the role. Instead of easing themselves into the role they want to hit the ground running. Pull all the SLT and high potential talent together and collectively design a strategy that they all buy into. This gives the new Leader a great opportunity to get to know the team, see them perform, see who puts oxygen into the room and who drains the room. The leader is also sending a clear message to the team that they want to tap into what they think, feel and believe to collectively design the go forward strategy. The Strategic Thinking process is brilliant for newly appointed leaders.

Key Takeaways

Critical Thinking means utilising analytical skills to evaluate and make judgements.

The quality of your thinking determines the quality of your thriving.

Every major technological revolution was driven by disruptions in the market by innovators who utilised Critical Thinking.

The businesses that utilised this Critical Thinking thrived during these previous revolutions.

To thrive in this current Fourth Industrial Revolution, your business must adopt Critical Thinking.

To engage in Critical Thinking, you must ask the right questions in the right order.

Great questions = great thinking.

I think it's important to note that Critical Thinking is a continuous process and not a 'silver bullet' with one great answer or solution. How many vacuum cleaners did James Dyson invent before he got it right and made £billions? (Answer: 5,127 prototypes… and a lot of Critical Thinking…)

Get Started

1. Reread the definition of "critical" and "critical thinking" at the beginning of this chapter and think of some examples in your life where you exercised Critical Thinking.
2. Find an area of your business that is causing you stress or worry. Work out the right questions to ask yourself about that area of your business.
3. Consider one or two of the organisations which are thriving today because they deployed critical thinking. Try to imagine the kinds of great questions each of them might have asked to get where they are now.
4. Finally, the flip-side. Think of two or three organisations who paid the ultimate price by *NOT* deploying critical thinking.

Engaging the Leadership Team

Leadership has less to do with you as the Founder, CEO, MD or Managing Partner than it does with **who** you involve in driving the Strategic Thinking in your business.

All great leaders involve their entire leadership team in Strategic Thinking.

Let's take a look at Henry Ford's quote again:

"Thinking is the hardest work there is, which is probably the reason so few engage in it."

I beg to differ.

The way to make thinking – and especially Critical and Strategic Thinking – simpler, you need to:

- Involve your entire extended SLT and
- Give them a framework, such as the one laid out in this book.

The sooner it becomes less about the CEO or "the boss" and more about *them*, the better for your company's growth.

The starting point on the Strategic Thinking journey has to be the engagement of the SLT to ensure their buy-In. I mentioned that without their buy-in the company's leadership might sometimes even go so far as to sabotage a strategy to prove themselves right, or to spite the boss for not involving them.

By engaging your leadership team, you allow them to **own the strategy,** which makes the successful execution of the strategy far more likely. In the final section of this book I'll share a very simple frame I call the Growth Grid which explains this principle in a bit more detail.

Many Heads Are Better Than One

I made a YouTube video on this a while ago and repeated the phrase, "It's not about *you*; it's about *who*."

And the *who* might indeed encompass more than just the leadership team. You might want to include some high-potential people in the organisation, or perhaps even some key decision-makers at the department level.

Make sure that every key function of the business is represented.

There are three direct benefits to involving the entire SLT:

1. The resulting strategy will be far better than if it had been designed by just you, the CEO.

2. By harnessing the entire SLT (plus others if appropriate) you're tapping into what they all think, feel and believe. This will definitely deliver a strategy more likely to outthink, outpace and outmanoeuvre your competition.
3. The team will also take a much more active role in ensuring it is executed. If they were involved in its design, they are invested in and committed to its success.

Some companies will have a senior leadership team of, say, ten people. But four of those people are on the board while the others aren't. Let's call these four the "big D's".

Too often, companies separate these people so that the "big D's" determine the growth strategy then ask the "little d's" to make it happen or at least have a critical role in delivering the strategy.

That's an error. It creates a divide. The "little d's" are less likely to buy into the growth strategy if they weren't party to its design. Also, why the heck wouldn't you seek to involve the wider group to accelerate their development and strengthen the pathway of succession? In addition of course you're tapping into what they think, feel and believe to make the output so much wider, deeper and richer.

Forget that antiquated method. Put all the d's and D's in the same room and have them bash out the strategy together. Put a few heads of departments and some stellar rising stars in there as well.

That's the way to produce the best outcome.

Corner Office Syndrome

Utilising many heads, and engaging your leadership team, is *the* way to avoid Corner Office Syndrome, which we covered in the chapter on the Nine Danger Signals.

Instead of the boss making all the decisions and telling everybody where to go, engaging the wider leadership team means that the burden is shared and the team decides *collectively* where they are, where they want to go and how they're going to get there.

The formula is:

Your team + the Strategic Thinking frame + facilitation + the execution frame = great outcomes and an excellent growth strategy.

It's like a three egg omelette. The three eggs, the Strategic Thinking frame, the facilitation and the execution frame. You bring the ingredients – *your people and what they think, feel and believe.*

Now, everybody knows you can make a perfectly acceptable omelette with just two eggs. But there's a reason why great cafés around the world specify a "three egg omelette" on the menu. The end product tastes better and is just so much more solid and filling.

Key Takeaways

Leadership has less to do with you and more to do with *who* you engage.

Strategic and Critical Thinking are more straightforward when done in a team, using the correct framework and facilitation.

More heads are better than one.

Don't split the team, bring big D's & little d's and rising stars all together. The final strategy will be better for it and the team will be more invested in ensuring it is ultimately successful.

Engaging the leadership team helps prevent Corner Office Syndrome.

Get Started

1. Work out who in your company you could bring together to create your organisation's 3-year growth strategy. Don't limit it to the most senior members of your team. Make sure every key function of the company is represented. Make sure people who really understand the environment and the customer are present.
2. Consider when this event could take place. Our experience of over 3500 Strategic Thinking Programmes suggests that the minimum amount of lead time for the two-day workshop is three weeks.

Who has the Answer?

Most consultants in the world are what I would call "content consultants".

Scan the QR code for this chapter's video

They get called in to help solve a specific challenge or to help take advantage of an emerging opportunity. They will *find out the answer for you*, then give it to you. They will take a brief on some problem the company doesn't know how to solve, or on some new great opportunity that they don't quite know how to attack.

Whether they're a big well known consultancy or a small niche boutique firm, they'll say, "Don't worry. We'll look into it, and we will *tell* you what to do." They'll talk to lots of people inside and outside the business, and they will come up with a proposal on how you can solve that problem or take advantage of that opportunity.

They then *give* you their answer. They'll give you *the content* for the plan of action.

There's nothing particularly wrong with this approach *if* that's what the leadership team is looking for. In fact, if the SLT is certain that the necessary know-how is missing, then absolutely the right thing to do could be to draft in that missing expertise or capabilities. A great example of this is bringing in a firm like SustainableX to help you craft and execute a strong sustainability strategy. Why on earth would you attempt to DIY a way forward when you don't have the width and depth of know-how needed.

I'm highlighting the situation when the CEO engages with a generic consulting firm to help get some clarity. No matter how it's communicated it feels like a vote of no confidence amongst the SLT.

That sinking feeling comes from the fact that what the CEO is really saying is, "I'm not convinced you guys will deliver the plan I'm looking for, so I had to hire an external company to come and do it for you. A colleague once remarked to me that "it's like getting slapped in the face with a wet fish."

It breeds insecurity and often resentment amongst the SLT, which in turn will definitely lead to a lack of SLT buy-in for the strategy. (See SLT buy-in.) If your SLT isn't truly bought into a strategic plan, they're not engaged with it and its chances of success are massively reduced. The only exception, in my view, is bringing in consultants or experts who have the required capabilities that the SLT perhaps do not. For example, know-how in sustainability, AI, machine learning, social selling, purpose, vision and values etc. For sure, this is when the content specialists come into their own.

We have no answers at all

Process consulting is entirely different, and this is why I bought into the business and set up DPI Europe in 2014 (now trading as peer2peer). Our core purpose is to train and enable leadership teams to improve the way they think and interact with each other, and to enable them to master critical thinking. We make them the centre of all thought generation and ideas. This is the complete opposite of the "Content Consultants" who will go to enormous lengths to make themselves the aggregation point of knowledge and insight. You've heard of the expression – "knowledge is power" – I'm sure this expression must have been coined by a senior partner of a large content consultancy practice. They make sure that all insight and knowledge roads lead to themselves. That they are the all-important aggregation point.

We are the consultants with no answers. We have no answers at all. We only have questions. But, crucially, the *right* questions.

No-one understands your business and your business arena better than you and the wider SLT. You may not have all the answers, but you should know where to look. This book helps you understand what you don't know.

That's the key required to open the door to Critical Thinking.

I passionately believe that you and your people have the answers. The role of the Strategic Thinking (ST) frame is merely to unblock that thinking. Our job is to unlock those answers and pull them out, to get you to walk down "Growth Street" and to arrive and complete "Game Changer Close".

The ST process is a journey, not a destination. It harnesses what SLT *thinks*, *feels* and *believes* about the business and marketplace and channels it into an excellent, game-changing growth strategy for the business. This is your destination.

There's a "famous" quote which makes its rounds on social platforms, even though no one knows who said or wrote it. It has been ascribed to a phantom teacher called "Alexandra K. Trenfor", and although we have no idea who this person is (or if she ever even existed), the quote is a powerful one:

> ***"The best teachers are those who show you where to look, but don't tell you what to see."***

Key Takeaways

Content Consultants give you answers and honestly should only be deployed if you have significant knowledge gaps. For example, if you need to make your packaging more responsible and sustainable, bring in a packaging expert who can help you evolve towards a considerably greener packaging range.

Bringing in generalist content consultants to do the thinking for your SLT will fuel resentment and ultimately never works because the SLT isn't and will never be aligned and behind the strategy.

Process consultants have no answers. They have the right questions in the right order.

You know your business better than anybody else. Only *you* have the answers to what your business and market need in order to succeed.

Like an awesome pie or cake, this book can be sliced up. Slices can be used individually as well as a whole sequenced event.

Get Started

1. Think of a time when someone came to you and told you that they were going to bring in an outside consultant. How did you feel?
2. Imagine you were bringing in a facilitator to orchestrate the Strategic Thinking process amongst your extended SLT, to help unlock Critical Thinking. Who would you involve in your organisation? Which high-potential rising stars from the "next wave" of talent would you include?
3. How would you inform the team that you were bringing an external into your business? How would you avoid the "slapped in the face with a wet fish" feeling? Perhaps use the omelette metaphor?

Part 2

The Current Business Model

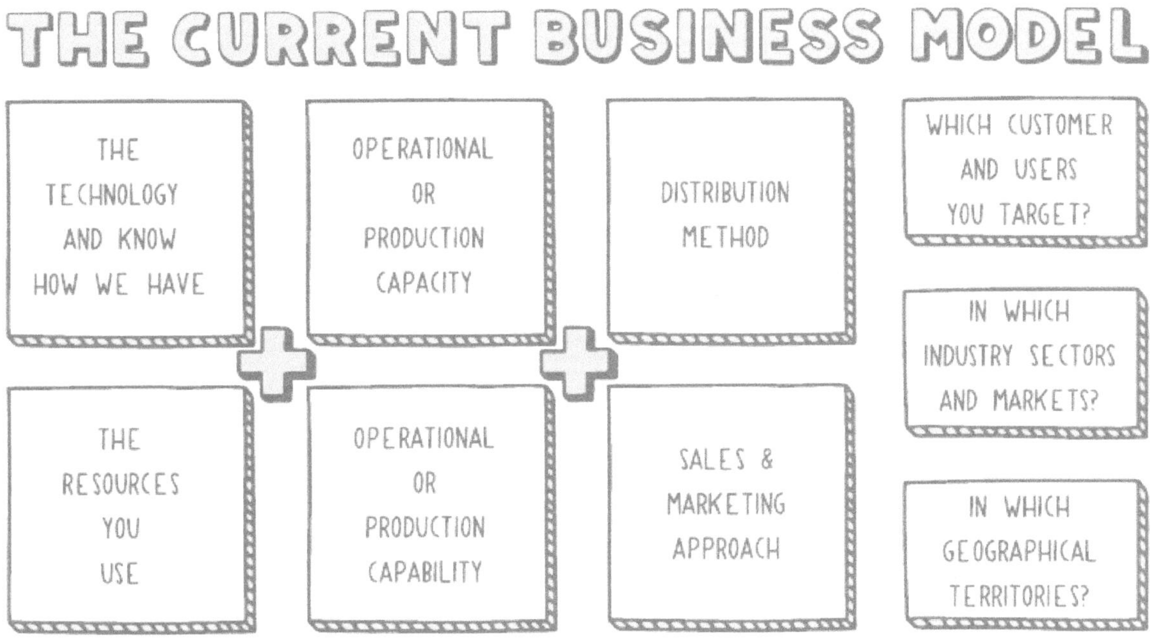

Fig 2.1c

Understanding your current business model is one of the fastest ways you can have a real impact on improving & growing your business.

A lot of people believe their business is straightforward. They think it's about developing a really cool product or service, finding customers who want to buy it and then *selling* it to them.

In essence that's true. However, if it was truly that straightforward few businesses would fail. Rolling 10 year statistics indicate that in the USA;

- 18.4% of start-ups fail in the first year
- After five years 50% have failed and stopped trading.
- After 10 years a staggering 65.5% have stopped.

Scan the QR code for this chapter's video

The basics of business are simple, but doing it well – surviving or better still being brilliant and thriving– requires a lot more thought and action.

These processes on how to master Strategic Thinking and how to effectively execute your strategy will guarantee a significant improvement in your business' performance.

A Novel Business Model Canvas

The concept of the Business Model Canvas is not a new one. I believe the initial design of what is generally known today as a Business Model Canvas was developed in 2005 by a guy called Alexander Osterwalder.

My version is different, but also, how and when you use it is different. I believe this framework can be used in two ways:

- To help the SLT review the current business performance at their regular SLT meetings
- Use it to aggregate the critical insights gathered during a major strategic review.

Instead of nine segments, as is usually used in the traditional Business Model Canvas, I believe that the frame of your current business model can be split into only **three** core areas.

1. How You Build Your Products and Services

To establish this, you need to look at:

1. The technology and know-how you deploy
2. The resources you have
3. Your production or operational capacity.
4. Your production or operational capability

The four points above, taken together, determine how you build your products and services which you bring to market.

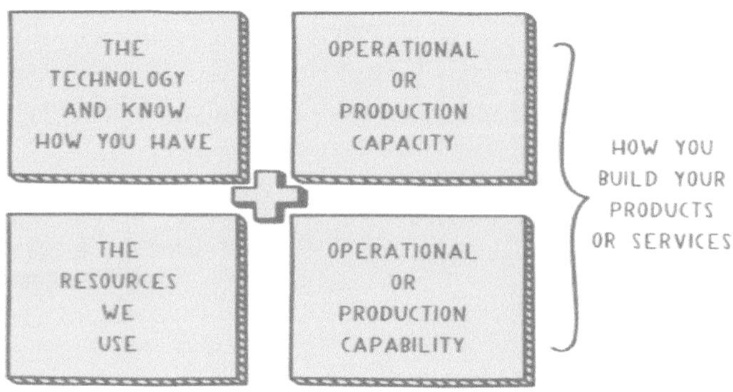

Fig 2.1.2

In order to use your current business model, you need to look at the above four elements and figure out what is working well and what isn't. What is inferior to your competition? What needs to be improved? Are the improvements "quick fixes" or would they require major system overhauls?

Let's take technology and know-how – You should be considering the effectiveness of any tech that is deployed in both product design and product or service development. Similarly with know-how – what IP do you have? What expertise do you deploy? How do you currently maintain or improve your know-how? Can you protect it and register it? Should you deliberately not register it and simply keep the formula a secret à la Coca Cola?

In terms of resources you should be looking at all materials you deploy in the production process or in the provision of your service. This can be physical materials such as wood, paper, energy etc., but equally people.

Concerning operational or production capacity – this is self-explanatory, I think. What capacity does your infrastructure have? For example, if you're a hotel it will include bedrooms broken down by size or by facilities, restaurant tables and cover capacity and in the spa the treatments offered and capacity, and so on…

Operational and production Capability is specific know-how or expertise that you have available as part of your capacity. For example, if you're a printer it might include specialist equipment that gives you additional capability to the standard print proposition offered by your immediate competitors e.g. security printing. If you operate a luxury spa it might be a specially heated room to offer hot yoga. You get the idea.

Delve deep into each of the four points above to establish precisely where you are currently. Consider establishing focus groups of all stakeholders to discuss what's working and what isn't.

It's important to realise that you're not currently looking at your future business model i.e. what it needs to be in the future, or what needs to be reshaped in order to accommodate our future strategy. That comes later in the book. We're reviewing the current business model in order to optimise and improve it. So our current strategy can be delivered even more effectively. In this respect this can be done as a one-off exercise.

All we care about now is understanding every issue and opportunity concerning how you build your current products or deliver services, what can be fine-tuned and improved. It is also necessary to review all support activities and how they might need to be evolved or improved to keep pace and contribute to future growth.

2. Who Are You Selling To?

The next step is to understand *who* buys your products and services?

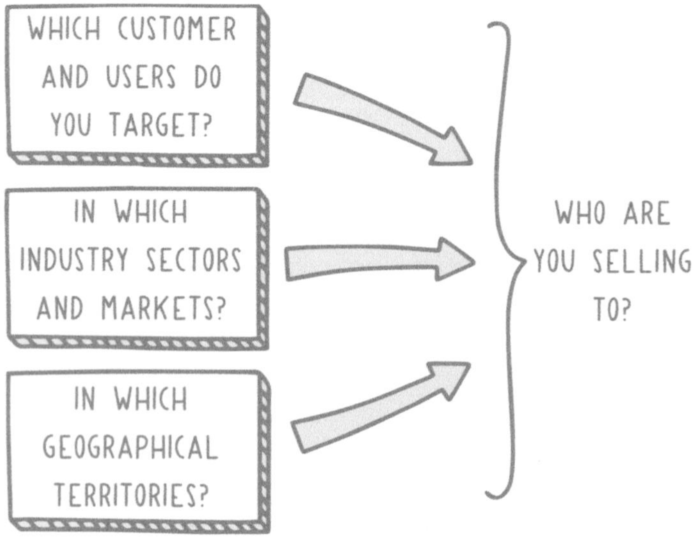

Fig 2.1.3

Who are you selling to, or who do you want to sell to?

1. Which customers and users will you go for?
2. Which industry sectors and markets will you target?
3. In which geographical territories will you operate?

It's important to understand that a customer is not necessarily the same as the user. A customer is who you sell *to, if you like, it's the person who pays the bill.* The user is the person who actually uses the product or service. Often it's the same person.

A company selling children's backpacks will have parents as its customers. But its users are the kids who will actually *use* the backpack and come back to their parents either complaining about or lauding the product's design and durability. That said, it's more likely that the parents will praise its durability. ;-)

Industry sectors and markets are identifiable groups of customers. For example, you might be a SAAS service provider to school business managers, who will be classified as customers. Whereas high schools, infant schools and universities might be specific sectors or markets.

Geographical territories are obvious. Depending on your business, it could be confined to a number of streets in a town, or towns in a county, counties in a country, countries on a continent, or globally. I urge you to be as precise as possible. Look at your delivery schedules. Look at your 80/20 rule.

Once you've established the above, only then can you begin to develop your sales and marketing strategy, and your distribution strategy. This is the 3rd area of our current business model frame.

3. How Do You Sell and Distribute Your Products and Services?

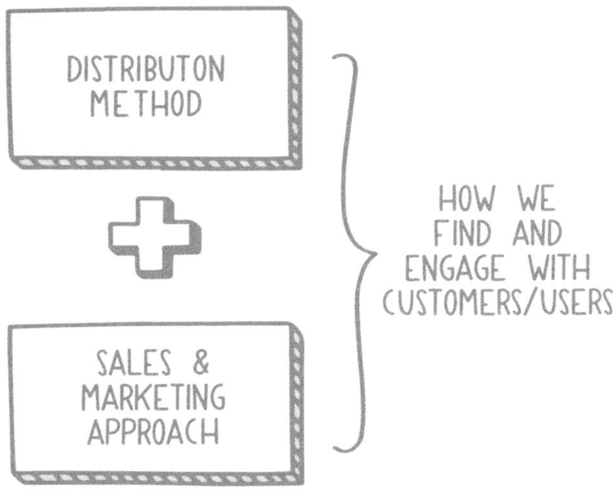

Fig 2.1.4

Distribution is how you deliver your products or services to the customers or users. It could be directly, through an owned branch network, through third parties etc. Consider the logistics involved. Consider alternative delivery partners. Consider who you could collaborate with to give you cost or reach advantages. What could be improved?

Sales and marketing is a massively important part of the business model. Understanding what's working effectively and what's not is critical. Your marketing and sales teams should never be afraid of challenging the status quo and questioning the sacred cows. I've seen many organisations where Sales and Marketing functions are at odds with each other. They've two separate leaders who are either adversarial or too cosy. Equally, I've seen many organisations where sales and marketing are combined. The issue here tends to be that, whichever function the leader ascended through, they are subconsciously or overtly biased towards. Achieving the optimum mix within marketing and sales is a critical challenge. Constantly reviewing and modifying is key.

The main point is this: In this chapter, I'm encouraging you to *take a look* at your current business model. Analyse each aspect of it using this simplified version of the Business Model Canvas.

And, through doing this, identify quick wins and ways to improve it.

4. The Consequences and Results

The final part of establishing the current business model is to determine the consequences or results of the first three steps.

1. What is the final revenue you're going to have?

2. What will all of the above cost?
3. What will the ultimate financial return be?

A Good Starting Place

When deciding on a strategy for your business, with the current business model you can utilise our simplified version of the Business Model Canvas.

You could simply use it as part of your SLT meeting. Use the frame to review what's going well and what needs to improve in your business right now. It will help you focus on the essentials and the dependencies between key areas of the business model. It will encourage the leadership team to think less in silos. It'll grow their knowledge, understanding, empathy and engagement with each other and other functional areas.

Equally, the current business model has been used as part of the two day Strategic Thinking workshop. It's a great framework to assemble all the critical observations that are fleshed out by the leadership team on day one of the process. It's especially relevant for;

- Current Profile
- Sandbox
- SWOT+

Key Takeaways

Using the current business model is a great tool to review regularly how the different elements of your business are working together or not....

The current business model is an excellent framework to do a quick assessment of where you stand as a business.

Future business models are only done *after* the new strategy has been worked out.

Get Started

1. At your next SLT give everybody the current business model frame the week before and ask them, with some of their team, to complete it from their perspective. Can you get them to consider what works well and what's not working so well.
2. Discuss all the responses and produce an agreed aggregated version.

Current Profile – Success and Failure

Every business or organisation has a current profile. That is to say, what products and services does it sell to which customers and users in which industry sectors and in which geographical territories. Your current profile is like a picture taken at any given time. It captures exactly what business you are at that moment. This profile will change and evolve over time. That's why it's called a *current* profile. What's really important is that SLTs should habitually regularly review what's working well, and equally what's not working so well regarding a business's current profile. Learning from these "success" and "failure" insights is critical. Regularly reviewing your current profile to evolve it so that you outpace and outperform the competition will underpin your success as a business.

Scan the QR code for this chapter's video

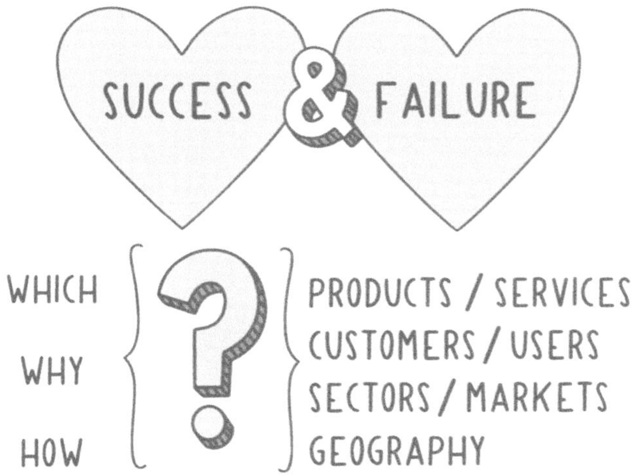

"Every great artist has a closet full of bad paintings."

That's another one of those great, pithy quotes which you'll find on the web and yet nobody knows who said it.

But it's incredibly relevant.

Now, before you think this is going to be another one of those TED Talk-style pep talks on "everybody has to fail a hundred times before they succeed", it's not. I'll leave that to all those performance coach experts.

What sets a great artist apart from a failed artist is that the successful artist learned from *both* their successes and their failures. Business is just the same.

As covered in detail in the Critical Thinking section, it is absolutely vital that you regularly and continually ask yourself *challenging questions* regarding your business profile.

But instead of just putting up a flipchart and writing down what went well this year, I advise that you adopt a more structured approach. Remember, great questions = great thinking.

Here are **twelve questions** in specific areas which you *must* ask yourself regularly in your business. My recommendation is to consider reviewing from now going back two to three years max. Many clients I work with will review the previous 12 to 18 months.

The Twelve Questions of Success and Failure

1. What factors determine whether a product or service is successful? Which products and services are successful? What caused this success?

The starting point has to be what outcome you are looking for to determine whether a product or service is successful. Whether it's sales revenue, gross margin, fewer returns, highest customer NPS (net promoter score) or even products or services that generate loads of social buzz, it's really important you decide what KPIs indicate why one product or service is considered more successful than another. Also, the weighting you apply to these KPIs might change over time. For example, if you've recently invested significant capital building capacity to fuel the growth of your business, you'll be likely to give significant weighting behind sales volume and revenue, and less emphasis on gross margin.

Once you've established your success criteria you can now determine which of your products or services are successful, and then ask yourself *why* they're successful or what caused this success.

What can you learn from that exercise? It's really important to capture the lesson learnt. Clearly, going forward you want to incorporate lessons and insights into your thinking.

2. Which products and services aren't successful, and why not?

Conversely, look at your less successful products and services and ask yourself why *they* aren't successful.

Does a particular product or service elicit more complaints? Or cause you to lose more customers than another? It might be a specific value added to a product or service, which in fact isn't adding value or is only adding tiny additional value but for significant cost and/or effort. Why?

What can you learn from that? How can you fix it? How could you stop it from happening again?

3. What factors determine whether a customer has been more successful than another customer? Which customers are more successful? Why was this?

Remember, customers and users are not necessarily the same. A customer *buys* your product; a user *experiences* it. Keep this in mind. It may be appropriate for you to ask the same round of questions about your users.

You might consider some of the following as success criteria:

- Spend levels are increasing significantly.
- The amount spent is high.
- They might be less price sensitive.
- They might buy a complete range of your products or services.
- They might buy significant quantities or a new product or of a strategically important product or service.
- They might be "contra seasonal" i.e. they trade up when most customers trade down.
- They might be more loyal or vocal advocates of your brand.
- They might regularly give you valuable feedback.
- They might rarely complain……

Try and describe that customer. Try and build a profile or avatar of them that embodies the type of customer that tends to tick more of the success boxes than others.

And, again, the key question to all of these: **What can you learn from that?** You'll need to take these learnings forward when you start to formulate your growth strategy. Some examples you might want to keep in mind later could be:

- Where do similar customers/users hang out so I can find more like them?
- How can I lock these specifically awesome customers down?
- How can we leverage these loyal advocates?
- How can these supporter users help us design better products going forward?

4. Which customers have we failed? Why do we consider that we failed them? What caused this failure?

Unless you're extremely fortunate, you cannot please all customers and users all of the time. Because you have identified what criteria measures successful customers, the flip side should be fairly straightforward to identify. For example;

- Spend levels dropping significantly.
- They're consistently spending very little, they haven't even covered the cost of sale.
- They're always looking to shave more and more off the price, we're entering zero margin/loss territory.
- They only buy one product and this is a product we're phasing out
- They might use your service only during two weeks of the year, and it's your busiest two weeks.
- They might be serial complainers, for no material reason other than that they just love complaining.

It's important to learn from this rich vein of insight. This is *"Innovation gold"*. How can you improve your proposition? Your systems and processes? The way you engage with customers and users? Again, remember to carry all of this awesomeness forward for when you are formulating your growth strategy.

Consider 'what can be done to remedy the situation?' If nothing can be done, would you consider developing a filter for these customers and others like them, preventing them from even signing up or buying your products in the first place?

5. Which industry sectors are you most successful with? Why do you consider them successful? What caused this success?

It's important to remember that a **customer has a pulse**. A customer is an individual you can describe and point to.

An **industry sector** is a collection of customers that make a body or group that you can describe.

Are there some industry sectors or groups of customers that are more successful than others?

Your criteria for judging success is likely to be similar to that which you used to measure customer success

Let's say that a business sells to doctors, dentists and pharmacies. Of those sectors, some will be less price-sensitive than others. Make fewer complaints, pay on time, be growing at a much faster rate etc..

In which industry sectors are your products more successful? Where do they just seem to work, and why?

6. Are you not so good in a particular sector?

Are there some industry sectors or groups with which you struggle to really nail the perfect customer experience?

In which industry sectors do your products tend to have more problems?

Why is that? And, what can you learn and adapt to improve that?

7. Do you perform better in certain territories?

Are there certain geographical territories where your proposition is more robust than in other locations?

Why is that? What can you learn from it? How can you improve your overall geographical reach for your products and services?

8. Do you perform worse in certain Territories?

Conversely, are there geographical areas in which your performance is weaker? Is it because you are not present in those areas? Or, perhaps, because you do not have enough resources there? Perhaps competition in that area is stronger or more relevant?

Perhaps your deliveries run better in the middle of the country, but not so good further up north. This goes back to the Business Model Canvas, working out your distribution based on who you are selling to.

Ask yourself *why* those areas are underperforming. And always ask yourself what you can *learn* from this, and how you can make it better.

The Two Most Important Questions

Once you've painted a vividly clear picture of your successes and failures using the above eight question areas, you can do the most important part:

You can **paint a fresh picture**, in other words create a new current profile. This new fresh profile will reflect the valuable insights giving your business a much greater chance of success, shining a light on what you need to do to achieve greater success and improved growth.

Equally as important, you now have a greater understanding of why you failed in some aspects. Do you address the issues and go again? Or do you focus on where you win and concentrate on winning bigger? In most cases, it makes sense to adapt the new current profile to eradicate the failures from your offer if at all possible.

The essence of this chapter – and you no doubt noticed that I repeated it often – is *what can be learned* from both your successes and your failures.

Lots of motivational speakers talk only about learning from your failures. But what many of them will get you to do is focus on learning from the big mistakes, the train crashes. What I'm trying to flag here is that it's more nuanced than that. Your business' profile is all about the products and services you sell, to certain customers and users, who reside in certain industry sectors or clusters in selected geographical territories. That's where you should start. *What worked and why? What didn't work and why?* And perhaps most importantly, *what can we learn from this to take forward into our strategy?*

Keep it simple. Follow the frame to analyse your **current profile's successes and failures**.

Don't Guess

Who you ask the above questions of is critical.

Don't *guess* at each of the questions. Go and look at the data. Speak with the stakeholder groups involved.

Key Takeaways

The Strategic Thinking process is about *asking the right questions.*

A good starting point is understanding exactly what your current profile is.

Then get into the recent successes and failures of your current profile.

Capture all the critical lessons learned and carry them forward into your strategy.

You're not necessarily looking for some massive failure to learn from or a random success to repeat. It's about exploring all aspects of your current profile and learning from what worked and what didn't work.

Get Started

1. Assemble a cross-functional team of your people who have the insight and reach to understand your success and failures.
2. Create an environment where they feel comfortable and engaged to honestly share what they think, feel and believe.
3. Go through each of the eight success and failure question areas and consider the answers to each one.
4. Record the successes and why. Identify how you might be able to leverage these successes and scale the plan rapidly. Equally, decide whether you learn from the failures and decide whether you stick or twist. Or, in other words, have another go with an improved approach or abandon it completely.

Know Your Sandbox

We need to clarify our terms again.

The last 20 years has fogged up the meaning of "sandbox". It is commonly used to mean a "test playground" for software developers to test their code. It's a controlled environment for businesses to experiment and innovate. It is a space where businesses, start-ups, or teams can test new ideas, products, strategies, or technologies without the risk of major failure impacting the core business.

Scan the QR code for this chapter's video

That is *not* the definition we are using here.

We're talking about that big box of sand – some people call it a sandpit – that, as kids, we used to hang out and play in with buckets and spades.

A sandbox.

Now, what does that have to do with business?

Everything.

What Is Your Business' Sandbox

Just as when you were a kid you chose to play in a sandbox, so do businesses.

Your business chooses to play in a sandbox. In this sandbox there are many other players or stakeholders. Understanding who they are and who the influencers are is absolutely critical. Think of a sandbox as a business' **"extended marketplace".**

Let's take a real-life example: Montblanc.

I've never worked for Montblanc. But, from the perspective of a professional outsider looking in and watching their business evolve, this is what I saw.

Once upon a time, Montblanc used to compete in the "luxury pens" sandbox. They competed alongside a handful of other high-end premium Pen producers successfully from around 1910 to 1977. It was a relatively small, but exclusive sandbox. This luxury pen sandbox will have had its own dynamics, its own rules of engagement and its own set of influencers. For almost 70 years, Montblanc will have measured its success against the other players in this sandbox.

Then, in 1977, Alfred Dunhill Ltd acquired Montblanc. The new leadership team probably recognised that in order to grow the business they needed to compete in a different sandbox. They entered the luxury gifts sandbox, probably identifying a new customer and user within its new current profile. They now plotted a course to target specifically **"successful business executives".**

The new sandbox gave them a much broader competitive landscape but also gave them a much bigger opportunity to expand their revenues. Their current profile changed completely. Over time they transformed their product range. They extended their distinctive logo to many different gift items. They now produce aftershaves, perfumes, watches, briefcases, cufflinks, document cases, wallets, belts, even headphones and of course, very nice pens. They target international business executives, so they adjusted their distribution and their sales and marketing strategy to include having a retail presence at every significant airport, everywhere in the world.

In the example of Montblanc we can see the transformational impact of going from one sandbox to a larger sandbox. In 1993 when Swiss-based Richemont Group acquired the brand, they continued to solidify its position in the high-end premium luxury market.

It's easy to see how changing your sandbox can change your business trajectory completely. But it's not just about changing your sandbox. The other option is to better understand the one you compete in right now.

Success and growth doesn't necessarily have to come from moving into a larger sandbox. It is also very possible to achieve significant success and growth from going the opposite way and niche down into a smaller sandbox. It's often easier to build a strong reputation and be a significant player in a smaller niche sandbox.

For example: when I was putting this book together, I coincidentally did a pro bono Sandbox Workshop with a pet food manufacturer in the south of England. They're a great little company called Nurturing by Nature, family-owned, and have grown at a dramatic pace. They make dog and cat food only out of natural raw ingredients – no chemicals, no artificial preservatives, just natural stuff. And they've managed to come up with products that are affordable.

So, their *users* are the dogs and cats themselves. But their customers are the *owners* of those dogs and cats.

But who else is in their sandbox?

You have:

- Regulators
- Suppliers
- Retailers & Distributors
- Competition
- Media and Promotion

Regulators – who sets the rules and regulations for the industry? They could be directly regulating i.e. food standards, or indirectly regulating, for example Health and Safety.

Suppliers – where do they source the raw ingredients from? Can they tie them down to exclusive deals? Can they identify a USP through their supplier farms?

SPEND MINIMUM
50% OF YOUR
TIME LOOKING TO
THE FUTURE.

Retailers are an essential element of the sandbox. Who do they target to stock the raw natural pet food? They may look beyond the obvious pet shops or local supermarkets for example – garden centres, whole food shops etc. How do you get them to stock it? Can they get their products on Amazon Marketplace and pet related online sales websites? Could they consider franchising raw pet food high street shops?

Competition – consider the direct competitors who also produce fresh raw pet food, but also those from the mainstream Pet Food sandbox. Customers may choose to revert to perceived lower price options. Equally customers could decide to "DIY" and source their own raw food from local butchers. Perhaps consider other new entrants e.g. if Hello Fresh or local farm shops entered the raw pet food business arena. They need to keep an objective perspective on all these possibilities.

Media and promotion – Who are the social influencers on Facebook? Instagram? Outdoor events, Crufts, Lifestyle magazines, YouTube. Is it worth advertising on social media sites such as Facebook, a big draw for cute pet videos or running a pay per click campaign on Google, sponsoring something at Crufts etc.

Amongst all of the stakeholders in the sandbox which ones exert *influence?*

Without doubt **veterinarians** are significant **influencers** in the sandbox. If they could become engaged with the benefits and affordability of Nurturing By Nature's Raw food range, that could be an absolute game changer.

Indeed, how could Nurturing By Nature become an influencer themselves in the media and promotions piece? Perhaps by aligning themselves alongside some social influencers. Perhaps they could partner with local dog trainers or with local cat hotels or even pedigree dog and cat breeders.

Do you see how the word "market" doesn't even begin to cover the scope of your business' sandbox?

By understanding your sandbox, you'll get greater clarity of view about who sets the rules, what the rules are, and how you could possibly change the rules.

By knowing your sandbox, you might even gain clarity on an adjacent sandbox that might be more attractive for your business. Or you could cross promote your sandbox.

Why the Sandbox Isn't Your Marketplace

If you were to put a hundred CEOs in a room and ask them to talk about their marketplace, they would talk about the industry sectors, geographical territories that they target and the customers they sell to.

They probably wouldn't talk about the social influencers, suppliers, distributors, regulators and everything else that impacts on that marketplace.

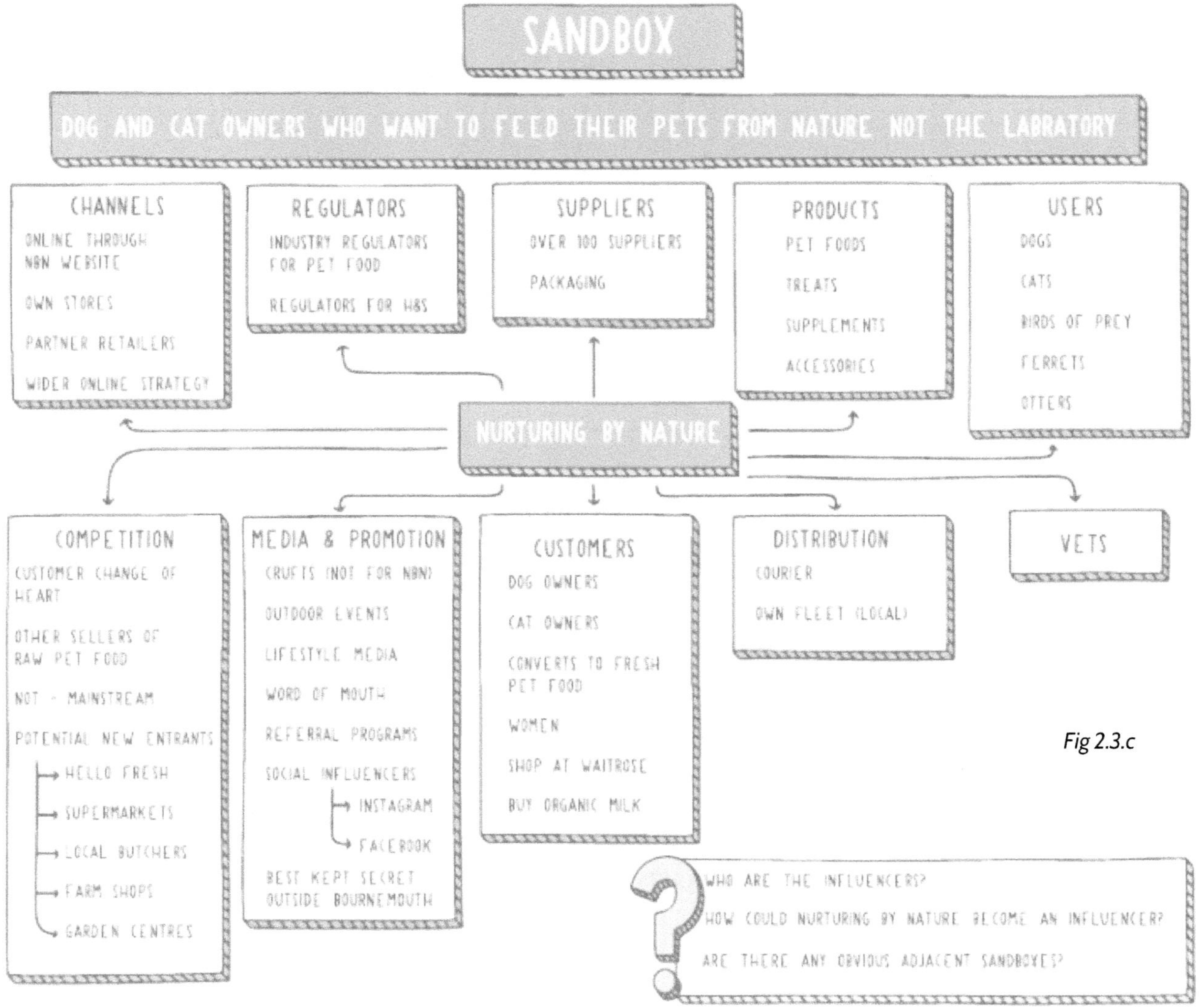
SANDBOX
DOG AND CAT OWNERS WHO WANT TO FEED THEIR PETS FROM NATURE NOT THE LABRATORY
CHANNELS
ONLINE THROUGH NBN WEBSITE
OWN STORES
PARTNER RETAILERS
WIDER ONLINE STRATEGY
REGULATORS
INDUSTRY REGULATORS FOR PET FOOD
REGULATORS FOR H&S
SUPPLIERS
OVER 100 SUPPLIERS
PACKAGING
PRODUCTS
PET FOODS
TREATS
SUPPLEMENTS
ACCESSORIES
USERS
DOGS
CATS
BIRDS OF PREY
FERRETS
OTTERS
NURTURING BY NATURE
COMPETITION
CUSTOMER CHANGE OF HEART
OTHER SELLERS OF RAW PET FOOD
NOT - MAINSTREAM
POTENTIAL NEW ENTRANTS
HELLO FRESH
SUPERMARKETS
LOCAL BUTCHERS
FARM SHOPS
GARDEN CENTRES
MEDIA & PROMOTION
CRUFTS (NOT FOR NBN)
OUTDOOR EVENTS
LIFESTYLE MEDIA
WORD OF MOUTH
REFERRAL PROGRAMS
SOCIAL INFLUENCERS
INSTAGRAM
FACEBOOK
BEST KEPT SECRET OUTSIDE BOURNEMOUTH
CUSTOMERS
DOG OWNERS
CAT OWNERS
CONVERTS TO FRESH PET FOOD
WOMEN
SHOP AT WAITROSE
BUY ORGANIC MILK
DISTRIBUTION
COURIER
OWN FLEET (LOCAL)
VETS
WHO ARE THE INFLUENCERS?
HOW COULD NURTURING BY NATURE BECOME AN INFLUENCER?
ARE THERE ANY OBVIOUS ADJACENT SANDBOXES?

Fig 2.3.c

That's the sandbox. It encompasses far more than just your "market", per se.

We should think of the sandbox as an "extended marketplace", *way* beyond just your customers, users, industry sectors and competitors. Or consider that a sandbox is a 360 view of the **entire landscape of stakeholders.**

Sandbox Influencers

More needs to be said about this because it's often overlooked.

A perfect example is when a baby is born at the hospital.

When the proud parents and their newborn leave the hospital, the parents will usually receive a bag of "goodies" – nappies, nappy rash cream, some baby formula, some wet wipes, etc.

The products there are almost certainly always going to be from the Unilever or Procter & Gamble stable.

These companies have identified that the hospitals and medical team are massive influencers over new parents. They recognise that midwives are a *massive* influencer group for the mums and dads.

The midwife is prohibited from endorsing your product, but he/she *can* give you a bag with either the Unilever wet wipe in it or the Procter & Gamble one. Given the huge pressure on health service budgets, having large corporations donate key essentials to form part of a newborn baby "starter kit" is very much welcomed.

Once the initial gift supply is about to run out, mum or dad will go to the supermarket, it's almost guaranteed that they're going to buy the same brand, even if it's more expensive, because they might be worried not to do it.

The midwife and other medical professionals are massive influencers.

Imagine I go to the vet and say, "Well, my dog doesn't seem to be eating her food." The vet turns around, grabs a bag of "Super Duper Dog Food+ Ultra" and hands it to me, then says, "Well, try feeding her this!"

If my dog then does eat it, what do you think I'll buy the next time I go to the supermarket? It doesn't only have to do with the fact that she ate it (although that certainly helps). It has plenty to do with the fact that a *Sandbox Influencer* pointed me in the direction of the product.

This is a vital concept to know and understand for your business success.

Sandbox "Rules"

Your business sandbox has rules.

I'm not referring to regulatory or legislative rules, although those certainly also exist. I'm referring more to the rules that people seem to subconsciously follow.

This is best explained through an example: let's talk about the world of taxicabs before Uber.

If Uber, an unknown at the time, was looking at the sandbox for cabs, they'd see that there were a few rules in place.

How did people hail a cab before Uber?

One way was to go to a hotel and the hotel would have a queue of cabs outside. Alternatively, you could go to a taxi rank.

In this case, the rules are being set by the city council – where the taxi ranks can be, how they're allowed to operate, and so on.

Some cities allowed the cab to cruise with the light on and you could hail them down, but not all cities permitted this. In other cases, only the licensed cabs could do it and not the minicabs.

But the hotel doorman might also be setting rules. He/She might have some special agreement with the cabs, or perhaps even a special light they switch on which indicates that someone needs a taxi, instead of having the cabs queue up outside, clogging up the entrance and detracting from the hotel's ambience or prestige.

Uber looked at this sandbox and decided, "Well, we'll empower the *customer* to be in control. And we'll do it with this handy device that everyone has in their hands – a smartphone. All the customer had to do was download an app, register and, boom, they were in control.

They've got cabs.

There was GPS in the cab, and the customer can see this in the app – more empowerment.

Uber entered the sandbox and changed all the rules.

The city council attacks on Uber – perhaps from pressure from the black cabs (London) or the Yellow Cabs (New York) – are well-publicised. These city councils tried to take Uber on.

Uber is an excellent example of looking at the sandbox and then changing all the rules.

Other examples include Airbnb, Apple iPhone, SouthWest Airlines, Tesla, Netflix, Spotify and PayPal – there are so many.

Changing Your Sandbox

Earlier in this chapter I talked about Montblanc changing its sandbox. Montblanc was probably the market leader in the sandbox of luxury pens once upon a time. (I don't know this for a fact, but if you asked me for any other brand of luxury pens I wouldn't be able to give you so many names – so they certainly imprinted their branding on me personally.)

That's a pretty small sandbox to be in.

Today, they work in the luxury gifts sandbox as part of Richemont Groups €2.6bn luxury segment sales in 2023. They may well have an even narrower description of their sandbox, e.g. luxury gifts for successful executives and frequent travellers.

I've never spoken to anyone at Montblanc about this, but my guess on what happened is this: They thought, "You know what, if we want to significantly grow this business we need to *change the sandbox* that we compete in. So, which sandbox can we go in?"

The way to do this is to look at some adjacent sandboxes – it's easier to take a small step up into a larger sandbox or niche down into a smaller one than it is to take a transformational leap.

So, Montblanc stepped next door into the luxury *gifts* market. Their competitors would change – they'd now be competing with the likes of Gucci, Cartier, Hugo Boss, Tag Heuer, Louis Vuitton, Hermés etc. depending on each product line.

This is an example of moving into a larger sandbox. Sometimes it makes good business sense to move down to a smaller sandbox, where perhaps you can be a bigger fish, a greater influencer. An example could be a dental practice that decides to focus purely on cosmetic dentistry. Or a marketing agency deciding to focus purely on social media selling.

Key Takeaways

Your business' sandbox is far more than just its "market". It encompasses much more than that.

Make sure you know who the influencers are in your sandbox.

Every sandbox has rules.

Sometimes, it's possible to enter a sandbox and change all the rules. People refer to this as becoming a game-changer.

It's also possible to move from a smaller sandbox into a larger one. In this case, it's best to look around for sandboxes that are nearby. It's easier to take a step rather than a leap.

Equally, it's possible to move to a smaller sandbox. Go more niche.

Get Started

1. Look at your business and work out what sandbox it's in.
2. Write a descriptive short statement or sentence to describe your sandbox.
3. Then, work out who is in your sandbox:
    a. Competitors
    b. Distributors
    c. Retailers
    d. Influencers
    e. Suppliers
    f. Your people
    g. Anyone else you can think of
4. Write down some of the "official" and "unofficial" rules applicable to your sandbox.
5. Who are or who could be the influencers?
6. Can you become an influencer?
7. If not, can you influence the influencers?

To Compete or Not to Compete?

No company has the resources or the ability to compete with every single competitor out there.

In business, you need to *choose* your competitors, ideally before they choose you.

Even not-for-profit companies and charities compete. They're competing for hearts & minds and wallet share.

Scan the QR code for this chapter's video

You have no choice regarding whether you must compete or not. What you need to do is *choose your battles* and understand your competitive landscape better than everybody else.

You need to be intelligent about your competition. You need to understand what they're doing and compare it with what you're doing. You need to try and outthink them and deliver a superior customer experience and/or better value.

This chapter is all about how to be *proactive* about your competition, and not fall into the dangerous habit of simply passively reacting to your competitors or to your competitive landscape. Drive the agenda, be an influencer, dictate the game. Choose your competitors, before they choose you.

COMPETITOR ASSESSMENT V'S OURSELVES

	A-	B-	C-	D-
STRENGTHS				
WEAKNESSES				

Fig 2.4.1

Understanding Your Competitive Landscape

No matter your size – whether you're a small, medium or a large business, you need to understand who your competition is and then choose who you're going to compete with. To succeed, you can't just blindly compete with everybody out there. You need to be selective about who you compete with.

Let's just think about this for a second.

When you go into business, you are producing or delivering something that you want people to buy. Very rarely you'll find yourself in a brand new sandbox that you've created. Even in this scenario where no competitor currently exists, it won't be long before adjacent sandbox players take a look over the fence and join you. So let's assume it's an established sandbox with incumbent competitors. Your customers will be looking to compare your offer with the competition whether you recognise it or not. They'll examine your relative offer to theirs and decide which product or service they'll buy.

So, don't be apathetic and passive on this one. Take time to evaluate precisely who you want to compete with. Think about whose offer you are most likely to better. Who's too cosy and comfortable and has taken their eye off the ball? Who's the one with the declining reputation?

Once you've selected who you're going to compete with, you then compare your proposition, your service or your product, pricing etc. with these competitors.

For example, Fiat doesn't compete with Porsche, Bentley, Rolls Royce or even, to some extent, BMW. Fiat might compete with Renault, Citroën, Ford and so on.

For Fiat to take on Porsche would take a complete reinvention of its entire business model and brand. They'd probably have to acquire another brand much closer to Porsche, for example Aston Martin.

Fiat, therefore, designs its products with an exact sandbox and competitive landscape in mind.

Another vital thing to understand about the competitive landscape is that there are two distinct types of competition:

- Direct
- Indirect

Direct Competition

Direct competition is usually more obvious to spot.

Direct competitors are those who offer the same or similar products or services that you do, e.g. Ford and Renault, Holiday Inn and Ibis, Tesco and Sainsbury's etc. You can also have direct competitors who compete for a specific product or service range e.g. in the mobile phone arena, Apple and Samsung, or for Intra European flights, British Airways, Lufthansa and Air France.

Back in the day (for those of us who remember it), it used to be Nokia and Motorola.

You can also have way more than one direct competitor e.g. Ford competes with Renault, but also Vauxhall, Nissan, Fiat, Volvo, Toyota, Kia and so on.

I'm sure you can think of plenty of other examples.

Indirect Competition

Indirect competition is less obvious, and can sometimes be quite tricky to spot.

Indirect competitors are those whose products or services are not exactly the same, e.g. Hilton Hotels and Airbnb. Each of these companies offers an entirely different proposition, and yet both offer beds and overnight stays.

In essence, their product is similar, it addresses the same pain or want, but the experience is entirely different. So different, that initially it's not immediately obvious that they're competitors. In spring 2025, Airbnb ran an extensive national TV campaign in the UK offering itself as an alternative to the likes of Premier Inn and Travelodge, particularly if you have growing teenage kids or if you're a group of adults going on a weekend break.

But, what about Uber and Fiat? What about Hertz or Six or Europcar or any other car rental and Fiat? What about bicycle manufacturers and Fiat? What about electric scooters and Fiat? If you take the perspective that it's about alternatives to getting from A to B., then suddenly it opens up a whole fresh view of competition.

As the world becomes more conscious of the environmental impact of motor vehicles, will they drop the car altogether and start riding bicycles, only renting a car occasionally when it's really needed? Indeed this is a rapidly emerging alternative car ownership model.

The *work from home* culture, which has become embedded in our society, at least in the immediate aftermath of COVID-19, could make this proposition even more likely. Why buy a car if you don't need to commute to work every day and just need one to take the family out for the weekend? Is the competitive landscape of car ownership changing to more of a pay-as-you-go model? For example, Zipcar or ONTO.

Perhaps to embrace alternatives e.g. scooters, electric bikes, public transport or a mix of these. This morning while walking the dog I was listening to the awesome Steven Bartlett's podcast – "the diary of a CEO". He mentioned that he'd recently sold his Range Rover Sport and replaced it with an electric bike.

All of these industries could be *indirect* competitors of a car manufacturer.

I mentioned Hilton vs Airbnb. The example is a somewhat obvious one.

Yet, both of these companies could have another potential indirect competitor: Any business selling products which promote a "staycation". Instead of spending their money on a holiday, people might instead spend it on a home entertainment system or better furniture for the garden, upgrading that BBQ etc. We're now entering the world of *substitution.*

Indirect competitors. Instead of spending their money on the hotel or Airbnb, folks are spending it on a substitute, alternative or a replacement.

Six Vital Questions About Your Competitors

How you view your competitive landscape is critical. There are some easy questions you can ask yourself, which will help you consider your competitive landscape more clearly.

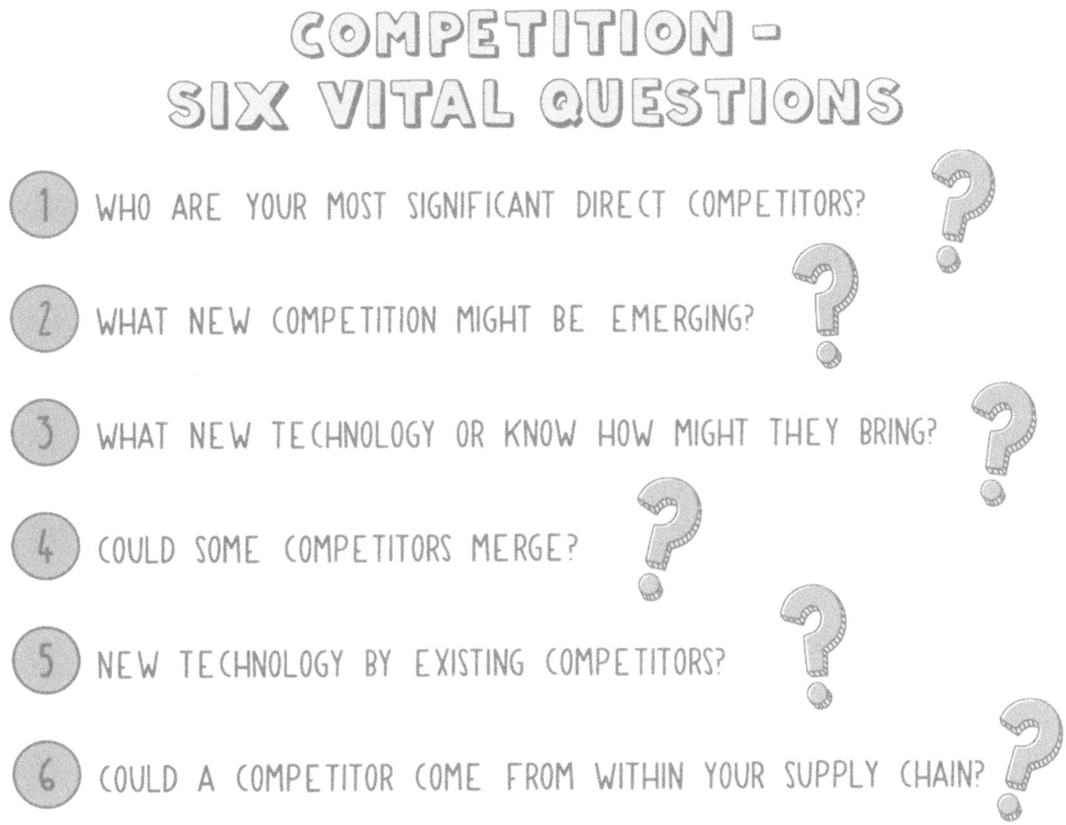

1. Who are your most significant direct competitors?

One way to answer this question is to see who your company has won business from in the last twelve months? Or, conversely, who you've *lost* business to in the previous twelve months?

This is perhaps easier to establish in the service industry where you invoice because you tend to deal with customers directly and then invoice them when you're done. However, if you're in the hospitality space, for example pubs, restaurants, cafés, etc, it's much harder to spot when a loyal customer switches allegiances to another local player. Equally, it's important to try and establish this for businesses dealing in products as well. Can you build in mechanisms or processes to track changes in buying habits due to new competitors?

One way to establish who you've lost business to is to do an "exit interview" if at all possible. Call them up and do a survey. Say something like, "I'm sorry you're going, but could I just ask you three questions?"

Try and find out who they've gone to instead of you. Why did they leave?

It's my experience that people don't often leave because of price. Sure, the price might be part of it, but there is almost always another underlying issue, for example the service has dropped off. Or the product keeps breaking, or your sales team said it was waterproof when it isn't etc....

One more essential point: We're looking for *significant* direct competitors. If you've lost one person out of a thousand to Company X, that isn't significant, unless of course this one client was responsible for 20% plus of your revenue, but, that's an indicator of another issue...

The significant competitor could be direct or a new, disruptive indirect competitor.

Only after establishing your significant direct competitors can you then proceed to do a meaningful strengths and weaknesses analysis.

In the "Critical Thinking: What? Why? How?" chapter, we mentioned how important it is to ask questions in the correct sequence in order to achieve truly effective Critical Thinking. We also used the example of a SWOT Analysis.

You *must* understand your competitive landscape and know *who* your significant direct competitors are before you can ever thoroughly analyse your strengths and weaknesses.

Ask yourself:

- What strengths do those competitors possess "relative to us"?
- What are their weaknesses "relative to us"?
- How could you mitigate these "relative" strengths?
- How could you exploit those "relative" weaknesses?

I recall in 2009 when I was CMO at DPD, our significant direct competitors included DHL, UPS, TNT and FedEx. We had a relative weakness versus all of them in terms of both brand recognition and Intra European Express services. They all had some 50 to 100 freight planes within Europe flying parcels overnight. We had zero. We depended on a very effective road linehaul system. I took the decision to flip this disadvantage into an advantage. We launched a carbon calculator tool and initiated a whole campaign around the environmental impact of flying parcels around Europe. Was it really worth saving perhaps one day in speed terms but emitting 10 times more CO2 per parcel? Central to this campaign was a new carbon calculator website called – www.whyflyparcels.com. This website allowed shippers to calculate what CO2 they'd save by simply switching to the slightly slower but significantly greener road based solution. The competitors were stuck, because they also had road based solutions, but didn't want to cannibalise revenues from their more profitable air express services. Then an "Act of

God" or *Force Majeure* kicked in – In March 2010 an Icelandic ash cloud grounded all internal flights within Europe for several days. We quickly mobilised and ran full page adverts depicting pictures of the grounded DHL, UPS, TNT and FedEx planes with a caption, "DPD, business as usual." This was a tipping point. Volume switched overnight from plane to truck, the dependability and sustainability arguments finally took hold. This was the start of DPD going from fifth in Europe to the #1 parcel player in Europe in less than six years.

2. What new competition might be emerging?

Whether direct or indirect, look forward a few years and see if you can envisage any new players coming into your sandbox.

A new direct competitor might appear in the form of a new regional office being opened up in your area. It could be a company that had always been in your geographic zone but suddenly becomes a major competitor as a result of a large investment into their business.

Ask yourself who the likely new direct competitors might be, as well as the new indirect competitors. However, try to think along a reasonable timeline. For example, if they're going to be a significant player within the next 12 months to 18 months. If they're unlikely to amount to a significant threat within a 3-year timeline then perhaps it's a watching brief only at this stage.

Sometimes, a technology breakthrough can lead to a sudden rise in direct or indirect competitors. A great example is Steven Sasson, a young engineer at Kodak who invented the first digital camera in 1975. Kodak, instead of embracing this breakthrough, tried to ignore and suppress it. All the Kodak Board could focus on was the cannibalisation impact it would have on the cash cow "film processing" business. It's highly likely that with the Kodak SLT the voice of the FD and the impact of cannibalisation was much louder than the R&D director. The rest is history.

Gather intelligence. Collect data. This is one of the key areas where I keep stressing the importance of involving more than just the SLT in your Strategic Thinking process. In this context, think about who in your organisation is likely to have insight into new indirect or substitute competitors? Analyse new information coming in and ask yourself, "What does this mean for us and our business going forward? How do we need to evolve, adapt, pivot, change as a result of this new breakthrough information?"

Are we investing enough into our future, studying market trends or increasing our R&D?

3. What technology or know-how would come with these new competitors?

The technology doesn't necessarily need to come from a competitor. New technology on its own might change the rules of the sandbox, such as in the example about digital cameras, which then generates new competitors.

A great example is video streaming, coupled with the large-scale availability of 4G and broadband. This technological change meant that people didn't buy movies in a box anymore, ie DVD's. Why would they when they can just download them or stream them directly to their devices?

This same technology changed the way music would be consumed. People now stream their music directly to their phones as part of a subscription model with Spotify, Apple, Amazon, YouTube or any of the other music streaming services.

For the leadership teams of Blockbuster, Our Price, HMV etc. etc., this was so predictable. The signs were clear and present for all to see. They could have acquired the breakthrough new platforms, but chose to ignore it. They simply did NOT deploy any kind of Critical Thinking. Indeed, you could argue they had a distinct lack of Critical Thinking.

Accounting is an industry in the process of being disrupted. Instead of paying an accountant to sort out Payroll, VAT and Corporate tax returns, many businesses now make use of cloud software such as Xero, Quickbooks, or FreeAgent or other cloud services to do their bookkeeping or to file their annual returns.

Accountants have had to adapt their services in order to stay relevant. Many now offer advisory services and are moving into the business coaching sandbox.

Charles Darwin said, "It is not the strongest of the species that survives, not the most intelligent that survives. It is the one that is the most adaptable to change." This is a very overused and over quoted piece of wisdom, but it's so true.

This is highly applicable in the field of emerging technology. Those businesses that adapt can survive. Those that don't, won't. COVID-19 had a devastating medium term impact on many industries such as hospitality, travel and tourism, events, live sports etc. These have for the most part bounced back completely, however, the long term impact on the "high street" and commercial office space could be permanent. Arguably, the pandemic has accelerated the evolution of the high street to an "experiential place". In other words, it has become a place where you experience stuff you can't get from Amazon. The rapid growth of ecommerce-related SAAS (software as a service) and logistics solutions is also massively contributing to the irreversible acceleration of the evolution of the high street.

The pandemic coupled with the evolution of video conference equipment and platforms such as Zoom and Microsoft Teams will permanently change the way people work and meet. They'll indirectly lead the repurposing of many commercial properties into residential ones. We are still observing the long-term changes in working behaviours and attitudes. In Q1 of 2025, many companies are taking a firmer line re WFH (work from home) and globally city business districts are getting back to pre-pandemic levels. However, the ripples have been felt in pension funds, house prices, the hospitality sector, even public transport utilisation and infrastructure expenditure. What will be the long term implications for the business district ecosystem? It looks like it's not as bad as first feared.

At the same time, it's vital to pass new technological breakthroughs through a filter and not go chopping and changing everything for every new piece of tech that shows up in your sandbox. Analyse new tech as it emerges, determine if it might or might not become a threat or lead to a *change in the way the game is played*. Then act accordingly. Do not bury your head à la Kodak, Blockbuster and Our Price.

The critical thing to keep in mind is whether any emerging technology, hard or soft, might change the competitive landscape or dynamics of your sandbox or business arena.

4. What about competitors merging?

The merging of competitors happens all the time.

The tech world and social media landscape furnish innumerable great examples like this one:

Facebook acquired Instagram in 2012 in an effort to beef up its competitiveness against Twitter and Google+.[2] They also acquired WhatsApp in 2014, making it even more formidable as a competitor to other social media giants.

Google bought YouTube in 2006.[3] Google purchased Android in 2005[4] , which was a total game-changer and, years later, allowed Google to enter numerous other sandboxes as a fierce and formidable new entrant competitor.

The tech world is rife with such mergers and acquisitions as the tech giants seek to gain more ground. Often driven by either the desire to take out an emerging new competitor or to "fast track" their own development by buying in know-how or tech. According to confidential emails released in 2018, this might indeed have been the very reason Facebook bought WhatsApp in the first place![5]

5. What about new tech by existing competitors?

This is when a current player or competitor launches some new groundbreaking, game-changing innovation that changes the rules. I recall UPS being the first to truly leverage driver technology in the logistics space with their DIAD pad circa 1991. They invested heavily in IT. employing thousands of developers. They made the DIAD the centrepiece of an aggressive long-term commitment to leading the way through technology. Indeed, their brand positioning evolved to being a technology business with delivery capability including a tagline – "we know logistics"

---

[2] https://www.cnbc.com/2019/09/24/facebook-bought-instagram-because-it-was-scared-of-twitter-and-google.html

[3] https://venturebeat.com/2006/10/09/they-did-it-youtube-gets-bought-by-gooogle-for-165b-in-less-than-two-years/

[4] https://www.nytimes.com/2015/05/28/technology/personaltech/a-murky-road-ahead-for-android-despite-market-dominance.html

[5] https://www.buzzfeednews.com/article/charliewarzel/why-facebook-bought-whatsapp

This was a game-changer in customer experience. The rest followed.

Another example from the same industry sector is when DPD launched their *Predict service* around 2009. Since then, DPD has systematically changed the game by focusing on tech to deliver outstanding customer experience to both the customer who ships the parcel and the customer who receives the parcel. Interestingly, UPS had been capturing the ETA per parcel several years earlier than DPD. But, they only used it for training purposes. It was DPD who saw the commercial benefits of providing this critical insight to both customers and receivers of the parcel. It took UPS years to grasp the commercial opportunity. By then, they'd lost so much ground in Europe.

6. Could a competitor come from within your supply chain?

Try looking up or down your supply chain. Is there an existing player who doesn't currently compete in your space today, but who could move into it from either up the supply chain or further down it?

Let's imagine you run a small chain of fruit and veg stores and then discover that one of the local farms has decided to open up a farmers' market in your area and sell directly to the public themselves. Or that farm chooses to offer a home box delivery service where your customers would get precisely the same fruit and veg, from the same farm, as you are selling to them.

Amazon is another excellent example (get ready for one of my many parcel delivery examples!). They used to use third party parcel delivery companies for all their deliveries. 100% of all their deliveries were done through parcel delivery companies.

Then, Amazon started developing its own logistics final mile fleet. *The Verge* reported in December 2019 that Amazon was, already then, delivering as much as 50% of its own packages.[6] The article reports them delivering 2.5 *billion* packages, placing it almost at the volume of FedEx, which delivered three billion packages a year.

In August 2020, CNBC reported that Amazon was now delivering nearly two thirds of its overall package volume itself.[7]

Virgin Atlantic provides another excellent example – when it started Virgin Holidays. Virgin has also started cruises, appealing to a much younger demographic who don't usually go on cruises which tend to appeal to older people. But, the brand confidence, the appeal and trust Virgin had amongst Millennials and Gen X meant a whole new market was exploring taking cruises.

Another localised example is when a small chain of three gastro pubs in the south-east of England decided to go in both directions of their supply chain. They changed their strategy

---

[6] https://www.theverge.com/2019/12/13/21020938/amazon-logistics-prime-air-fedex-ups-package-delivery-more-than-50-percent

[7] https://www.cnbc.com/2020/08/13/amazon-is-delivering-nearly-two-thirds-of-its-own-packages.html

and sourced all produce from within five miles of their pubs and no longer bought from cash and carry. They reduced their menu to a seasonal one with weekly specials. They also launched a business delivery service from kitchen to boardroom in less than an hour using their own fleet of electric delivery vehicles.

COCD

It's imperative that you avoid Competitor Obsessive Compulsive Disorder (COCD). This was covered earlier.

Remember the example I provided of Lidl and Aldi coming into the UK supermarket sandbox and completely changing the rules? It's important to remember that they did this by exploiting the very strengths of the Big Five players – their wide product range of 300,000 SKUs (stock keeping unit).

And their rise was meteoric in terms of public appeal to both discount shoppers, high end premium shoppers and everybody in between. The combined market share of Lidl and Aldi has grown from 8.5% in 2015 to over 17% in January 2025. Staggering.

When deciding with whom you should be competing, be aware of COCD. Don't fixate on just your major competitors or only a few competitors. Look wider and deeper. Who's changing the rules? Who's demonstrating agility and dynamism that's resonating with customers?

DIY – the curveball

Finally, before we bring this important section on Competitors to a close, I want to introduce you to a curveball. In many service-based sandboxes such as business advisory, bookkeeping, fitness, copywriting, web design, sales support, gardening and even getting your hair dyed, the first true competitor is DIY (do it yourself). This is when the customer decides to have a crack themselves. This could be driven by technology advances, know-how availability e.g. Youtube, online courses on kajabi or similar. Economic environmental changes can be a catalyst for the DIY explosion. The recent introduction of some serious AI platforms such as ChatGPT, Bard, Chatsonic, Jasper AI etc. are likely to have a serious impact on DIY competition.

It's always worth challenging your paradigm by asking the question – Can our customers elect to do this themselves, and have they already done so?

Go through the **Six Vital Questions** to work out precisely who you should be competing with, who might become a competitor in the future and who you can safely ignore for now.

Key Takeaways

If you're in business, you're in competition. It's not a question of "to compete, or not to compete", In business, you don't have a choice. But, believe it or not, you do have a choice about who you compete with. Go find them, before they come hunting for you.

Choose your battles. Try to choose who to compete with.

The best way to do this is to run through the six questions to compartmentalise your competitors and see who you are best placed to compete effectively against.

Get Started

1. Ask yourself the six questions to better understand your competitive landscape;
    a. Who are your most significant direct competitors?
    b. What competition might be emerging?
    c. What technology or know-how would come with these new competitors?
    d. What about future competitors merging?
    e. What about new tech by existing competitors?
    f. Could a competitor come from within your supply chain?
2. Now, write down who some of your direct competitors are.
3. Then write down who some of your indirect competitors are.
4. Choose which of these competitors you want to compete with.
5. Consider what adaptations to your current profile and business model need to take place. This will increase your effectiveness to compete.

Future Business Arena (FBA)

Do you remember the *Back to the Future* trilogy? Marty, Doc, Hoverboards, the iconic gull winged DeLorean…

For those of you too young to be au fait with such cultural classics, all you need to know to succeed in business is that the inventor who cracked time travel in that film (Doc Brown) used a DeLorean sports car as his time-travelling vehicle of choice. Even Biff, the "not so smart" villain of the film, was quick to recognise the incredible value of being able to see into the future.

Scan the QR code for this chapter's video

In business, it is equally incredibly valuable if you can lift the *fog of uncertainty* and see more clearly what's just over the horizon in your chosen Business Arena. Imagine for one moment if you were able to accurately predict what your Future Business Arena (FBA) was going to look like in the next six months to three years. Imagine the advantage it would give you and your leadership team over your more myopic competition,

Capital-intensive industries need to look much further ahead than the next 3 years – industries such as hospitals, hotels, motorways, travel infrastructures like railways and airports. Think and plan in decades rather than years.

If you're in the hotel industry, you wouldn't build a hotel based on what's going to happen in the next three years. You'd be looking at the next *twenty* years. To do that, you might need to look at birth rates, demographic shifts, emerging populations, changing habits, and so on.

Strategy is straightforward. It comes down to:

- "Where are we now?"
- "Where do we want to be?"
- "How are we going to get there?"

This chapter deals with "Where do we want to be?"

A key part of knowing where you want to be is that you need to get clarity on what changes might occur. You need to understand your FBA (Future Business Arena) – you have to understand what could be changing in the future landscape in which you compete.

Knowing this will help you decide how you can best adapt and position yourself in that future landscape.

The **FBA frame** allows you to remove the fog from your vision so you can see down the road and towards your destination.

Before we begin though, please be mindful of one important thing. **Look inwardly and outwardly.** That is to say look at your own business for sure, BUT, remember to look even harder externally under the six macro and six micro factors.

Uncertainty and Decision Paralysis

If you're uncertain, you're likely to fall into "decision paralysis" and pause any decision-making at that point of uncertainty.

This is human nature. Peter Fisk, the outstanding Marketing and Business strategist captures this issue brilliantly. I had the privilege of interviewing Peter when preparing this book. He believes there are two meanings for CEO:

- Chief Exploitation Officer – Milking today for what it's worth, focusing on cost cutting and tactical day to day management.
- Chief Exploration Officer – focusing on the future, with an innovation and expansive mindset.

Even the Chief Exploration Officers rarely make decisions in the face of uncertainty unless they're real risk-takers. Usually they'll wait for the fog to clear on its own, but by then it's often too late and the opportunity has gone by. Possibly, by that time, others have also come in and taken advantage of that lost opportunity they didn't take.

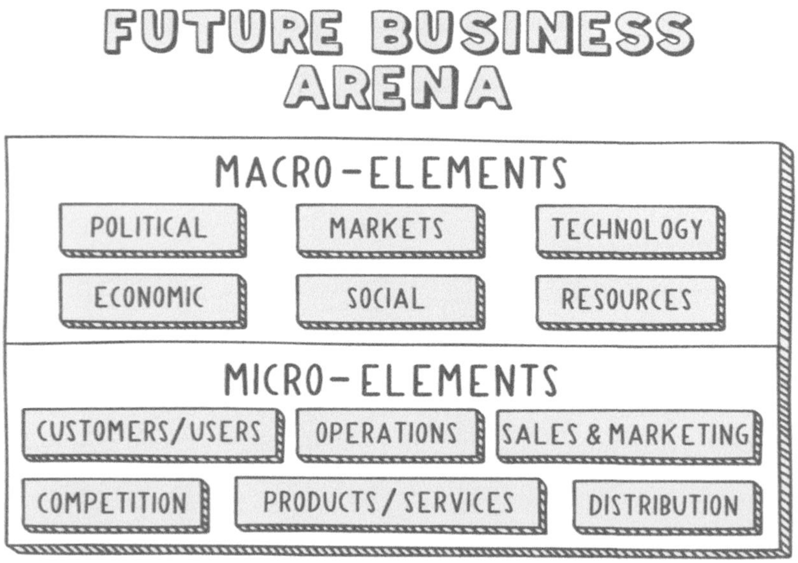

Fig 2.5.0c

There are **Twelve Elements** to the FBA. Six are **Macro-Elements,** and six are **Micro-Elements** which you can look at to assist you in clearing the fog yourself and so avoid decision paralysis in your business.

The Six Macro-Elements of the FBA

The Macro-Elements of the FBA can be loosely defined as things or events that are mostly outside of your control but which you must be prepared for and understand the implications or impact they might have. Once you know this, you can then adapt your strategy to take full advantage of opportunities, respond well to threats and mitigate any vulnerabilities.

1. Economic Environment

Look at what might happen with the economy in terms of things such as interest rates, buoyancy, employment rates, foreign exchange rates, cost of living, wars (which may affect supply chains), and pandemics. Do any of these things show indications of growth, contraction, or maintaining the same level?

What are the implications of the above for your business and the Business Arena specifically?

Let's say you're a premium-brand clothing company which designs and sells high-end suits.

If the economy changes drastically, those customers of yours who usually buy your brand or Hugo Boss or Armani *might* also decide to save some money and buy a suit from M&S during tough times. Instead of £1,500 on a suit, they'll spend £500.

Tough times mean more people are more likely to substitute premium services or products for more cost-effective ones. So, predicting the economic environment is quite important in establishing your FBA.

This book is being written during the aftermath of the COVID-19 crisis, the continuing war in Ukraine and President Trump's second and thankfully final term. Whilst the full extent of the global, regional and national economic impact is yet to be seen, it is fairly certain that huge swathes of buyers will be downsizing their expenditure, or delaying making significant expense decisions. Businesses will need to consider what support they can bring to help clients and customers spread the cost.

Does this mean that your premium suits business needs to start offering a mid-range suite of products? Or does it mean it needs to market more aggressively to high net worth individuals who might not necessarily stop buying expensive suits during such a recession?

Interest rates is another topic which is vital to keep an eye on. If you need to borrow money to scale your business, it might be too expensive to do it when interest rates are high, requiring you to "wait it out" a little until they go down again. Or you may need to deploy the support of funding experts to help guide you towards optimum source of funds. National Governments are working hard to offer grants and guaranteed loans to enable businesses to continue to fund innovation, expansion and growth.

It's important to look closely at the economic radar in the local geographical territories where your business operates. Look at the industrial sectors you operate in. Explore the economic situation of every key stakeholder in your sandbox. What are the implications? What actions could you take?

2. Political, Legislative and Regulatory Changes

Here's a perfect real-life example that is currently ongoing.

It is highly predictable that Europe will ban the use of single-use plastics in the next few years.

So, if you're the CEO of Evian or some other bottled water or soft drinks company, how will you get your product out there if that occurs? Most likely, you'll switch to more acceptable sustainable packaging options, for example cans or glass bottles.

Take a look back at plastic bags. Once upon a time you'd get those for free, then you'd have to pay tax for them. Now they've all but disappeared and shoppers are encouraged to bring their own multi-use shopping bags or pay to buy a plastic bag.

If you were the manufacturer of those bags you could have easily predicted that ban long ago as a significant possibility. How could you pivot and adapt? Could that manufacturer create plastic bags which are reusable or made from recycled plastic or other substances such as bamboo?

As for bottled water or soft drinks companies, could they come up with some kind of digital solution for their bottled water products? Could they add, let's say, NFC technology to a high-tech bottle so you could go fill up your bottle at various water dispensers located at each major supermarket? Perhaps such a dispenser would allow you to fill up any bottle, but if you had bought an Evian bottle, you'd get a discount. Will they simply revert to glass bottles? I'm not an expert in this field by any stretch. But I'm certain this is top of the agenda at brands such as Evian, Vittel, Lucozade. They have to find a more sustainable way of getting their product consumed.

Whatever they do, the matter of this plastic bottle ban is inevitable. It's only a matter of when. Companies who manufacture such bottles or use such bottles must be taking action now or their businesses will disappear. The soft drinks industry also faces the distinct possibility of increasing *sugar taxes*, which could be catastrophic.

As for political change, an excellent example is Brexit or the impending duty levies threatened by the Trump administration. Any international company that trades directly with the USA or other single market economies needs to keep an eye on duty taxes and barriers. It's so important to evaluate what the FBA is going to be like given these new or emerging challenges, both in terms of sourcing the materials they may need and the subsequent exporting of finished products.

3. Markets

How is your market going to change in terms of your competitive landscape, geography, industry sectors, etc.? Is the market going to grow? Tighten? Will it change shape?

GREAT QUESTIONS
IN THE CORRECT
SEQUENCE
LEAD TO GREAT
THINKING.

Consider between now and 3 years from now, what changes and adjustments might we anticipate?

For example, if you're a vehicle insurer, post-pandemic they had to consider if people would be using their vehicles *more* as a result of not wanting to share public transport. Alternatively, would they begin to use them *less* because they're now working from home more? Certainly, most heavy business mileage people I know initially did less mileage, but now are back at pre-pandemic levels. Yet, insurance is far more expensive than pre-pandemic rates.

This is leading to many individuals rethinking their relationship with the car. People might start calling up their insurers and saying, "You know, I actually don't need my insurance three hundred and sixty five days a year. I only go into the office on a Monday now. I want a flexible "pay as you go" kind of model to reflect this change in my lifestyle."

Some more traditional insurers might push back. But the more innovative customer-centric ones will look at it, see an opportunity, and say, "You know what? We're gonna change the game!"

Home insurance might change to include special cover for a home office insurance, thereby achieving a sort of hybrid between home and commercial insurance.

These are just some examples of how the market might change directly as a result of a significant global change.

You have to look at your market and how it might change.

Consider whether more or less regulation is likely to happen. What form might this regulation change take? And the implications?

Consider whether the market is ripe for consolidation or more fragmentation.

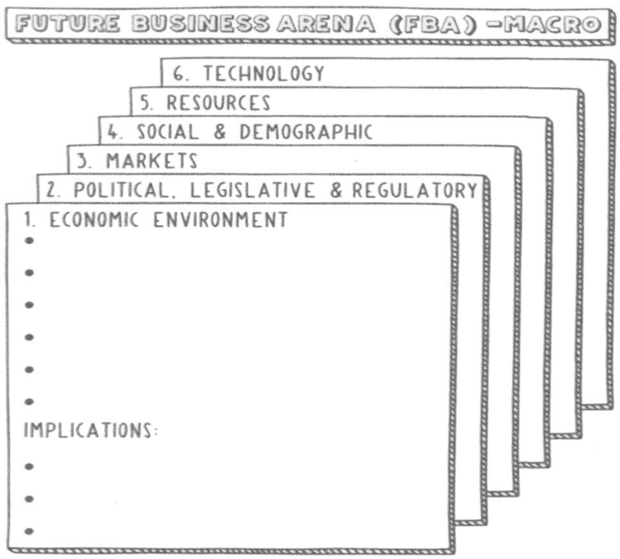

Fig 2.5.1c

4. Social and Demographic Changes

Social change is wide-ranging and touches many areas.

An ageing population is an example of social change that many people might not consider. People are also working longer hours these days; that's a social change. Many people now have multiple jobs and don't have the same perspective about lifetime careers. The job turnover is higher now. Much has been written by experts about differing mindsets to work amongst Millennials (born between 1980 and 1995) and Generation Z (born between 1996 and mid 2000s). Certain employers need to be very mindful of the increasing proportions of Millennials in management and leadership positions and Gen Z's growing numbers and influence around the place.

Right now, as I write this book, the significant social change with the initial mass movement to work from home has significantly reversed. Employers are now demanding employees come full-time back into the office. Earlier claims of no deterioration in employee performance have been significantly disproven. Other social changes that are increasing in impact for SLTs to embrace or be mindful of:

- Evolving Diversity, Equity and Inclusion (DEI) initiatives
- Less business travel as more work/meetings are done via Zoom and other collaborative platforms such as Slack and Microsoft Teams.
- Return-to-Office (RTO) mandates increase. That said, employee engagement levels tend to be higher if greater flexibility is shown.
- Gen Z are more focused on simplifying and having less stress, so fewer desire management hassle.
- Employee wellbeing and mental health increasingly impact on how employees want to be engaged with.

Social changes are slow to take hold and are usually very visible very quickly anyway – as long as you keep your radar switched on and facing the right direction. Sometimes, events can precipitate social change. For instance, COVID-19 accelerated a cashless society, resulting in everybody paying by contactless methods instead. It has absolutely accelerated the demise of high street retail as we've all turned to shopping online. It's accelerated the use of video conferencing as an accessible alternative to face-to-face.

5. Resource Availability

Money, people, raw materials – anything related to *resources* of any kind comes under this heading.

The availability of key resources for your industry has a massive impact on your ability to effectively produce your products or deliver your services. Availability could be temporarily stifled or, in the worst-case scenario, in global shortage. Keeping a constant watch and considering plan B or even C is wise.

With the massive global demand for electric vehicles (EVs) the affordable consistent availability of key components like Lithium or Graphite is key. Limited availability and massive demand for graphite or any other vital material will have a significant impact on price.

Another related example of resource availability in the EV space is charging points. Whilst scaling rapidly, at the time of writing this book the number of public charging points hasn't kept pace with EV new car sales.

In the logistics industry the most critical resource for several years has been people. Drivers are indispensable, whether that be last mile couriers or line haul truck drivers.

We can all recall during the COVID-19 pandemic the supply of PPE, face masks and even the little bottles which housed the vaccine proved to be a big challenge to source and supply. As the pandemic lifted there was a significant shortage of sea containers in Asia, which totally decimated the supply chain and led to huge supply chain challenges and long lead times, fuelling demand-driven inflation. Many western companies have since reviewed their whole supply and manufacturing strategy to look at "near sourcing".

What resources are key for your business? What is the short, medium-term availability and competition for this resource? You'll need to be creative in out-thinking the competition for the resource to make sure that you have all you need to fuel your growth.

SLTs may want to consider some of the following;

- Leveraging underutilised or non-traditional resources. Consider if there are any overlooked assets that competitors aren't looking at currently. So far as people are concerned consider more flexible staffing models for example freelancers, fractional execs, AI driven automations
- Harnessing data and insights better to streamline operations, improve decision making and resource allocation
- Exploring strategic partnerships or alliances perhaps with adjacent industries or non-competing businesses to create collaborative solutions.
- Changing mindsets to think more "ecosystem" and less isolationist. Look to build networks amongst a range of stakeholders.
- Finally, focusing on mindset and culture by rewarding inventive and creative thinking. Encourage entrepreneurial thinking.

6. Technology

More than ever, technology is moving at a faster, accelerating pace and most businesses can't keep up. As we've already seen in earlier sections, emerging technology can change the rules of a sandbox or Business Arena. It can ruin businesses who don't adapt, such as Blockbuster.

This was an example of new technology changing the way consumers consume. In 2004, if you were looking to watch a movie, listen to music or play a new video game, then visiting one of Blockbuster's 9000 stores globally was top of the list. At its peak in 2004, Blockbuster employed approximately 84,300 people: 58,500 in the United States and 25,800 in other countries. If you wanted home entertainment, going to Blockbuster was your default. However, with the advent of widespread broadband, advancement of smartphones, tablets and TVs combined with the emergence of streaming platforms, the end was very predictable. This was a great example of "business model transformation" driven by technology. Whilst the cases of business model transformation are increasing, the big issue facing almost every single business is "business model evolution" driven by technology.

Technology influences almost every aspect of your business. But, in 95% of cases, it's going to drive how your industry and specifically your company will embrace technology to evolve and improve your business model. Tech is driving the proposition, the processes that deliver the proposition and the way we engage with stakeholders – to a greater and increasing extent.

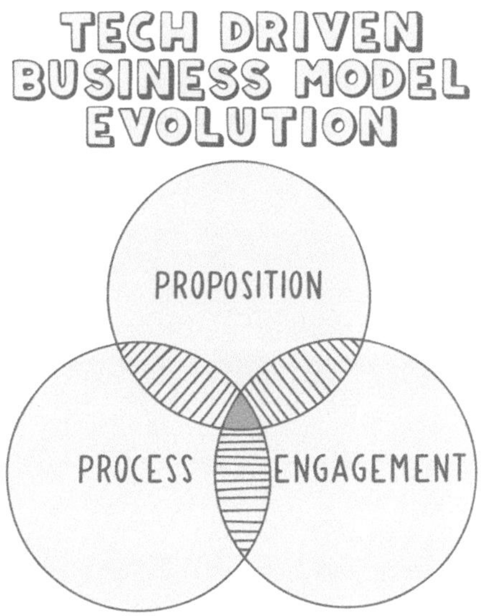

Fig 2.5.2c

Consider how technology could have an increasing role both in terms of hardware, software, platforms, insight, know-how and all stakeholder engagement?

AI (Artificial Intelligence) and RPA (Robotic Process Automation) are all the buzz in many industries today. For example, as accountants try to come up with ways to automate some of those many tedious tasks. Smaac is a German-based company which uses AI to automate people's accounting. Their system is supposed to teach itself as it goes along, getting better and better at its job.[8]

---

[8] https://www.thebalancesmb.com/is-artificial-intelligence-the-future-of-accounting-4083182

What does this advance in technology mean for accountants?

Salesforce and most other significant CRM platforms now use AI.[9] What does this mean if you're a CRM developer or a CRM support agency?

We're already seeing many examples of AI platforms being used to write copy, social media posts, undertake complex diagnostics and so on…

The examples are endless. Technological changes and advancements are significant and will undoubtedly have a massive impact on your FBA for the next two to three years. It is imperative for all SLTs to go wide and deep on how hardware, software and SAAS will be deployed in your business arena to transform or evolve the way business is done.

The Six Micro-Elements of the Future Business Arena

Micro Elements differ from Macro Elements in that they are more within your control. It's important to focus on what changes you think could happen to or within the Business Arena you compete in. Consider the whole arena, not just what your company might do or be doing. Don't get hung up on the labels for each of the Macro and Micro elements. You're essentially brainstorming by leveraging what you and your people think, feel and believe might happen during the next 3 years.

1. Customers and Users

Who is going to be buying or using your products and services in the future?

You are the one who determines your customers. Sure, they may come to you and buy, but you also choose to sell to them.

How could the buying behaviour of customers evolve? How will customers search for purchases? How important will product or service reviews be? Will certain accolades and awards hold increasing sway with buyers?

Let's imagine for a moment you're responsible for a chain of retirement assisted living accommodation. Your typical clients tend to be between 70 and 90 years of age. Historically, perhaps customers tended to be widowed, but perhaps an increasing number of couples are looking for a lifestyle change. Their requirements, needs and wants may be subtly changing, for example:

- They enjoy streaming videos and music, so want great broadband.
- Ditto for Zooming the grandchildren.
- They want plenty of charging points.

---

[9] https://www.softwareadvice.com/resources/salesforce-einstein-ai-primer/

- They want to know that green credentials are high.
- They love great-tasting coffee.
- They want to be able to come and go freely.
- They want to have a gym on site.
- They want to take part in activities like yoga, painting and pilates
- They don't want Monday night bingo as 'community entertainment', they're more likely to want Zumba classes and book clubs.

Can you see the emergence of new customer segments? Try to precisely visualise them as describable avatars. Remember you're trying to make educated judgement calls on what's going to change within the next 3 years for your industry's customers and users.

2. Competition

We covered competition in detail in the previous chapter and I make no apologies for touching on this again now. You cannot possibly take a forensic look at your FBA without including how the competitive landscape might alter.

You now know the difference between direct and indirect competitors. Do you foresee some new direct or indirect competitors appearing in the next two or three years? Ask those six vital questions regarding your competitors that we covered in the previous chapter.

Remember, it's not a question of whether or not you must compete, but a matter of *choosing* who you compete with.

The business you win and lose today, how do you see that changing in the near and medium future? What actions can you anticipate your competitors taking? Remember we are specifically interested in how we believe the competitive landscape in our Business Arena might change in the coming 3 years or so. Can we anticipate what behaviours and direction changes our competitors (direct and indirect) might exhibit over the next few months and years? Consider the following perhaps;

- Changes to pricing and the ways they may change their business models
- How certain competitors may adjust or modify their product or service offer
- How their leadership team or their recruitment strategy might change
- How competitors might adjust or tweak their marketing and sales or brand strategies
- What they might do differently concerning driving customer loyalty, advocacy and engagement
- Can we imagine that some competitors may collaborate? Or consolidate?

Lots to consider and reflect on. Remember, success is built almost entirely around how you and the SLT outthink, outpace and outmanoeuvre your competition. It's as simple as that. If you're successful here you will win and build a successful and thriving business.

3. Manufacturing & Operations

Whether you're producing products, providing a service or both, you will have operational, production or manufacturing processes and systems in play. So will your current and future competitors. So might your suppliers, customers and other stakeholders.

Advancements in the efficiency and effectiveness of these processes and systems could be key within your industry or Business Arena in order to sustain or evolve your competitive edge and position.

Consider: 'what changes are likely to happen within the next 3 years'? Have a look at your back-office processes and systems as well as how you manufacture or produce your goods. Consider how your service and ultimate customer and/or user experience could be improved through more efficient and effective systems and processes. You've just taken another look at the competitive landscape, what are they likely to do differently in the operation and manufacturing space? What would you do if you were leading that competitor?

Will you change to a more mechanised approach? Will you possibly take up an outsourced solution? In other words, outsource something to a specialist best-in-class supplier to enable you to focus on what you do best. Will you adopt a white-label system and start creating products for competitors? You might start to assess how some of the back-office stuff could be done in a more collaborative way by working with competitors to the benefit of all. You might even transfer some of your back office work abroad to countries such as South Africa, which is very proactive in this field and assists you in cutting your overheads considerably. You may think that local sourcing or insourcing is the way the Business Arena is heading.

The banking, insurance, security, pharmaceutical, postal, airline, education and many other sectors often collaborate to improve industry standards and practices across the sectors. Is this established or emerging as an option in your sector?

A few years ago, we worked with a client operating a network of car dealerships across the north of England. We worked with them to review its Future Business Arena as part of a two-day Strategic Thinking Programme. They realised that it's most successful and profitable competitor was starting to regionalise vehicle servicing in order to significantly streamline operations at each retail site. This would also enable the retail sites to focus on just that – selling cars and servicing. They discovered this when a service centre manager for the competitor applied for a job at one of their service centres. The leadership team concluded that they could also strip out a considerable amount of cost and offer a more efficient service solution for clients' vehicles if they migrated from a service centre in each of their 10 sites to two super centres providing the servicing for all client vehicles from all 10 of their sites.

A medium sized firm of accountants deployed our Strategic Thinking process recently. During the FBA session they realised two things were happening in their Business Arena:

- Accounting platforms were rapidly gaining traction across the board amongst SME and corporate clients and this was only set to accelerate.
- Being masters of several different platforms such as Xero, FreeAgent, Quickbooks, Sage and Zoho was no longer viable and was creating massive challenges in terms of keeping on top of functional changes. They were currently the jack of all trades and masters of none.

They surveyed clients and staff and concluded that they would specialise in Xero and recommend this going forward and become experts and extremely knowledgeable with Xero and its leading Apps. They would also support Quickbooks with the same knowledgeable focus. All clients would be "encouraged" to migrate to Xero, but, if they were on Quickbooks, they could stay with this platform if they wished to. This enabled them to achieve significant clarity and focus and ultimately offer clients a much better service going forward. They were able to reduce their cost to serve per client ratio and could cover more clients with fewer support staff.

Explore how players within your Business Arena might evolve and improve the efficiency and effectiveness of operations or manufacturing.

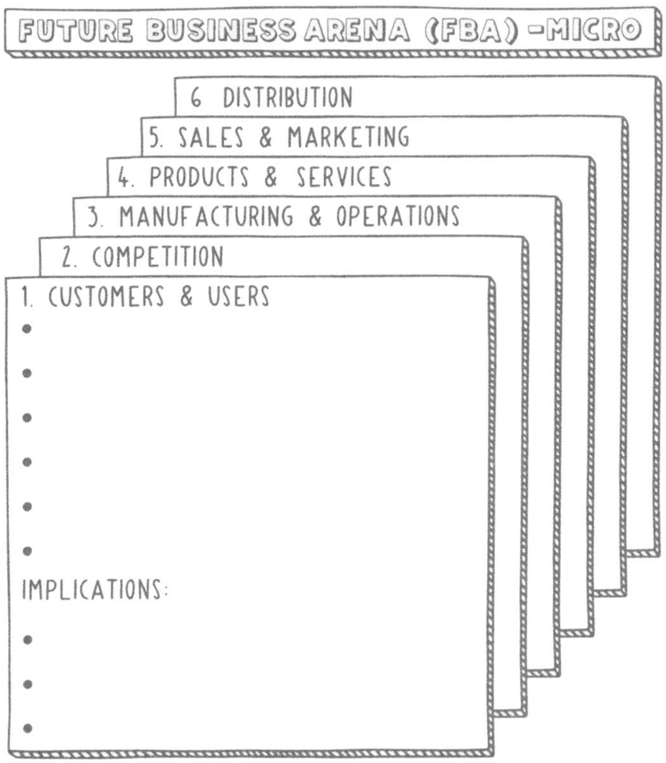

Fig 2.5.3c

4. Products and Services

Whether you offer products, services or a combination of the two, your offer is the resulting combination of your know-how, resources, capacity and capability. Within your chosen Business Arena, it's what your customers and markets buy. What do you imagine is going to change in terms of the products? Services? Solutions? What will be sold and bought during the next three years? You're looking for functionality changes or feature enhancements. Consider how customers might experience your service.

The banking sector has progressively evolved the way its products and services are sold over recent decades;

- 1980s – queuing in bank branches was a big issue. They evolved the use of cash machines: so that customers didn't need to enter the branch to withdraw cash, they used the "hole in the wall".
- 1990s – they realised that value came from cross-selling other services such as mortgages and other lending products, savings products, currency and travel insurance etc. But customers weren't entering branches anymore. OMG, what an own goal!!!
- 2000s – They redesigned the branches to become inviting comfortable places with ATMs inside, so customers would come in and they could cross-sell.
- 2010 onwards – it's all about digitising the banking experience and using apps and encouraging self-service.

This is a very simplistic view, looking from the outside in, to illustrate how a Business Arena's product, service offering and delivery can evolve over time.

Other examples include the office workspace market. Compare how Regus operated as the market leader for short to medium term flexible office space to how WeWork, Arena Business Centres and others have re-written the rule book and transformed the client experience. The latter – Arena Business Centres – is a client. Imagine if the Four Seasons hotel offered totally flexible work space – that's what Arena Business Centres is doing and they're very good at it.

5. Sales and Marketing

By understanding this, you could be the first one to do something really bold and really different regarding your marketing and sales in your Business Arena.

What do I mean by bold and different? At the St. Louis World's Fair in 1904, an advertising man by the name of William Cheever D'Arcy created a display for a Nashville distilling company by piping up water from the Mississippi river and building an eye-catching waterfall to promote the company's whiskey brand which was called Cascade Whiskey.[10]

---

[10] Frederick Allen, *Secret Formula: The Inside Story of How Coca-Cola Became the Best-Known Brand in the World*, Open Road Media 2015.

Look at how you conduct your sales and marketing. We've seen the massive impact COVID-19 has had on the way business meetings and sales visits have transferred to Zoom, Microsoft Teams etc. To coin a volleyball metaphor – will the market see a complete change in the traditional marketing "set-up" and sales force "spike" approach? I recently had a conversation with a guru in social selling (Adam Gray, take a bow) and he boldly claims that "marketing is dead and that the future is enabling and equipping all your staff with social selling skills". Then you've got the likes of Mark Ritson who is pioneering some outstanding, highly impactful marketing and running very successful mini MBAs in marketing online. He is never backwards at shaming lazy marketing and showcasing highly effective marketing. Wherever you stand on this, marketing and sales is changing at a phenomenal rate and it's vital that you assess what's going to happen during the next three years and stay ahead of the curve.

Look at what is going to change in sales and marketing and where you'll need to put more emphasis in the future. What do you anticipate your competitors doing? How can you improve the gathering and harnessing of data in order to improve prospecting and your customer experience? How can you introduce better marketing processes? Is there a place for sales funnels in your industry?

6. Distribution

Distribution is how you get your product or service to your customers and/or users.

Will you distribute through the cloud? Recent years have seen a massive increase in the number of online training programmes delivered virtually through the use of video and workbook combination.

I was able to deliver a very successful Strategic Thinking Programme to Soprema Group during December 2020 over seven, three hour Zoom calls over four days. At the end of the programme we received incredibly positive feedback. No doubt at all that the pandemic forced many service businesses to deliver digitally and many are continuing to offer this alternative post pandemic.

Will you partner with someone else? Will you adopt a licensing or franchising model?

Will you piggyback off someone else's infrastructure? A great example of this is Costa Coffee and how they partnered with BP to have a Costa Coffee self-service pod at BP stations across the UK, massively expanding the Costa Coffee brand reach, enabling them to scale rapidly in a single leap. For BP it gave motorists another reason to choose BP when refuelling – win win.

How might your competition go to market in a slightly different way? How might they choose to change the way they distribute their products or services?

Have you considered looking at industries and sectors reasonably close to you? Can you learn from how they're evolving? Can you hitch your wagon to theirs?

Distribution is a key aspect of your business model and the Business Arena you operate in. Yet, it is the one frequently overlooked by SLTs.

Key Takeaways

The Future Business Arena is all about looking at how the landscape might change, both through things largely outside of your control (Macro-Elements) and things much more under your control (Micro-Elements).

Whilst typically you should be looking at a three year horizon, some industries need to look far beyond just three years, for example incredibly capital-intensive industries such as hotels, airlines etc.

Uncertainty of the future can paralyse thinking and be the biggest cause of procrastination. Fear and risk must be counterbalanced through Critical Thinking.

Use the twelve elements of the Future Business Arena to do away with uncertainty. Start to formulate a clear view, based on some serious reflection, of how your FBA might change. Then consider the significant implications for your business in each of the 12 elements.

Even though you don't have Doc Brown's DeLorean, you *can* future-proof your business better than your competitors.

Get Started

1. Assemble a group of experienced stakeholders who between them have a good understanding of all 12 elements of the FBA.
2. You may wish to tap into the creativity and ideas of your next wave of talent, who are invested in the successful future of the business. The more ambitious the better as they will probably have a good idea on what is going on in the marketplace and especially in areas where you may not be so familiar e.g. social media.
3. Look at each of the six macro elements and six micro elements and consider each in turn. Try to predict what likely changes and evolutions are going to occur.
4. For each of the 12 summarise the key implications for your business.
5. Pick the most significant six macro and six micro implications. These 12 significant implications will be carried forward into designing your Future Strategic Profile.

SWOT+

Nearly everybody involved in business has heard of a SWOT analysis – an analysis of a company's Strengths, Weakness, Opportunities and Threats. It's one of the first things Business Studies students are taught at school or college. Many will also know that Strengths and Weaknesses are internal i.e. within your business. Whereas Opportunities and Threats are external i.e. they tend to be related to the environment or arena in which you operate or trade.

Scan the QR code for this chapter's video

So that's it, nothing more to be said. Well no, not by a long chalk. In my experience, very few people or businesses do a SWOT analysis correctly. That's chiefly because the way it's taught by either college professors or highly paid consultants is completely wrong.

The SWOT analysis, as it is often carried out in business, is hopelessly lacking in four key aspects:

1. It's all about the timing. It's often one of the first things undertaken by a leadership team during their fabled strategic retreat. WRONG, never ever do this first.
2. Depth is my next issue. Strengths and Weaknesses should not just be two lists, each one has to be divided into three subsets.
3. Weaknesses are not the same as vulnerabilities
4. Opportunities and Threats are not just what we see right now, it's also about anticipating what's over the hill and about to present itself?

A new acronym is needed to describe this entirely *thorough* and *comprehensive* method of conducting a SWOT analysis and I've settled on the abbreviation **SWOT+**.

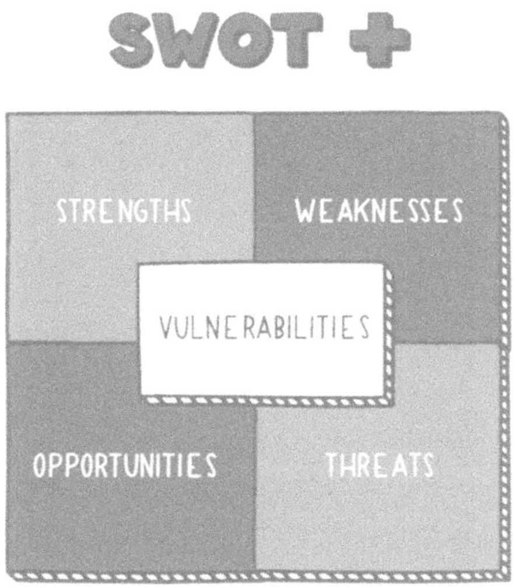

LEADERSHIP IS ABOUT WHERE AND HOW TO LOOK FOR OPPORTUNITIES, PRIORITISING THEM AND ALLOCATING RESOURCES.

Strengths and Weaknesses

Let's start with the timing issue – it is impossible to conduct an accurate assessment of your Strengths and Weaknesses in the absence of a full and complete competition audit of the kind we looked at in-depth in the chapter "To Compete or Not to Compete?".

Before even considering a SWOT analysis, and especially before looking at this section of Strengths and Weaknesses, you must thoroughly look at:

- Your direct competition
- Your indirect competition
- Potential new competitors coming into your space

And you must run through the Six Vital Questions About Your Competitors.

Think about it. Your Strengths are compared to whom? YOUR COMPETITORS. How can you possibly conduct an effective assessment of your strengths without first understanding who these strengths are compared with. This is exactly the same for your weaknesses. By definition it's your weaknesses vs your competition or a specific competitor.

Now for the second key critical aspect of doing a SWOT+ effectively. One of the terms we all see banded about very loosely is "your USPs" – your unique selling points. Most successful companies actually have only a few truly unique selling points or strengths. However, they will have shed loads of "relative" strengths (hopefully). In other words, relative to their competition many factors are stronger than the competition. These are the companies' relative strengths. So the first two subsets are "unique" & "relative".

Finally, and perhaps most difficult to flush out, is the third subset – your "latent" strengths. These are those unknown strengths and weaknesses that are lurking below the waterline. More about this in a moment. So the three subsets to Strengths and Weaknesses, which will give your analysis much more generous width and depth are:

1. Unique Strengths and Weaknesses vs Your Competitors
2. Relative Strengths and Weaknesses vs Your Competitors
3. Latent Strengths and Weaknesses vs Your Competitors

The key to unpacking your company's Strengths and Weaknesses is to:

- Do it after you've completed your competitor audit,
- Follow the three subset approaches and
- Assess vulnerabilities separately to weaknesses.

Let's take each one in turn.

Unique Strengths

If you own the patent to some unique gadget or process that nobody else has (or can have/copy), that is an example of a **unique strength**. It's something unique to your business.

This also applies to IP (Intellectual Property) or to some unique know-how, like Coca Cola's secret formula.

In Portugal, you can find these little unique custard tarts called *Pastéis de Nata* all over Lisbon, and indeed all over the country. And, yet, the original recipe for that *Pastéis de Nata* is known only to three people in the world – the original makers of the tart in a bakery in the city of Belem.[11] (At least this was true in 2017, according to an article in *The Independent.*)

That bakery has a unique strength, and if you've ever visited Portugal, you'd see that it is often packed with visitors wanting to taste "the original recipe".

Another example personal to me and my youngest son Enda: whenever we go to Anfield to see the mighty reds play at home, we always factor in enough time to visit the Golden Dragon Chinese Chippy. They have the most amazing chips and gravy. The owner fearlessly protects the secret recipe. As a result, on match days fans queue round the block. This is a unique strength.

Another example of a unique strength is if you have a key person of influence in your business, like Richard Branson and the Virgin Group. Or perhaps you've got a powerhouse celebrity signed up to endorse your product in all your ad campaigns, e.g. George Clooney and Nespresso.

A word of caution here is that celebrities are fallible and can soon swing from a unique strength to a vulnerability and then to a liability. for example Lance Armstrong (Oakley and Nike) and Kanye West (Adidas).

Unique Weaknesses

One example of a unique weakness would be if your business has less access to funding than your main competitors. That potentially puts you in a uniquely weak position if investment is key going forward.

Another example – when the Royal Mail and the Post Office separated following the Postal Services Act of 2011, the Post Office was now allowed to make its own independent strategic decisions. However, both were bound to use each other for the ensuing 10 years. This meant that as e-commerce drove the rapid expansion of PUDO (Pick Up Drop Off) points networks the Post Office couldn't open their network to other parcel carriers except Royal Mail. Similarly, Royal Mail had constraints on how they could partner with other PUDO networks. They both had unique weaknesses or strengths (depending on which lens you're looking

[11]https://www.independent.co.uk/life-style/food-and-drink/pasteis-pastel-de-nata-portuguese-custard-tart-recipe-secret-origin-baking-london-lisbon-a7839561.html

through). During a period of unparalleled opportunity, expansion and new competition, they both had their hands tied.

Relative Strengths

Whenever I do a strategic workshop with a business, I encourage it to name several competitors that it's going to compete with. Not only does this prevent the business from falling into COCD, but it also opens their eyes to an essential fact about **relative strengths** and **relative weaknesses**.

The fact is this: It might be that one of your relative strengths is relative only to one competitor, but is, in fact, a weakness when compared to a second competitor.

A strong board of non-executive directors might give you relatively better governance than one of your competitors. But a second competitor might have an even stronger board of advisers and NEDs.

It's important to look at these relative strengths and weaknesses both as a whole – relative to all the competitors you've chosen to compete with – as well as to specific competitors, in order to gain a full appreciation of your relative strengths and weaknesses.

One great example – back in around 2002 Dwain McDonald, former CEO of the DPD Group in the UK, launched an Aid for salespeople and customer facing staff. It was called "The Beat Factor" and its genius was in its simplicity. It illustrated how DPD stacked up against each individual competitor. Detailing the relative strengths and relative weaknesses, it went further and helped the sales guys to leverage the strengths and downplay the weaknesses. So, just prior to a sales call a sales exec would identify who the incumbent competitor was, gem up on DPD vs Competitor X and know exactly how to approach the conversation.

Also, it's important to keep in mind the ever-present reality of new competitors coming in, disruptors to the sandbox, game-changers. As best you can, you should evaluate your relative strengths and weaknesses against these too.

Relative Weaknesses

Exactly the same principle as with relative strengths. If you have half the number of branches or depots than your main competitors, that's a relative weakness in comparison to them. Or is it? In some contexts, having that capital overhead or being locked in to long term lease agreements could be a constraint. The migration to e-commerce was accelerated by approximately five years in one year in 2020-21 due to COVID-19. Having a massive retail network with enormous reach was perhaps an advantage pre-pandemic, but it definitely wasn't one during the pandemic and possibly afterwards. The message is simple, through different lenses relative strengths can be relative weaknesses.

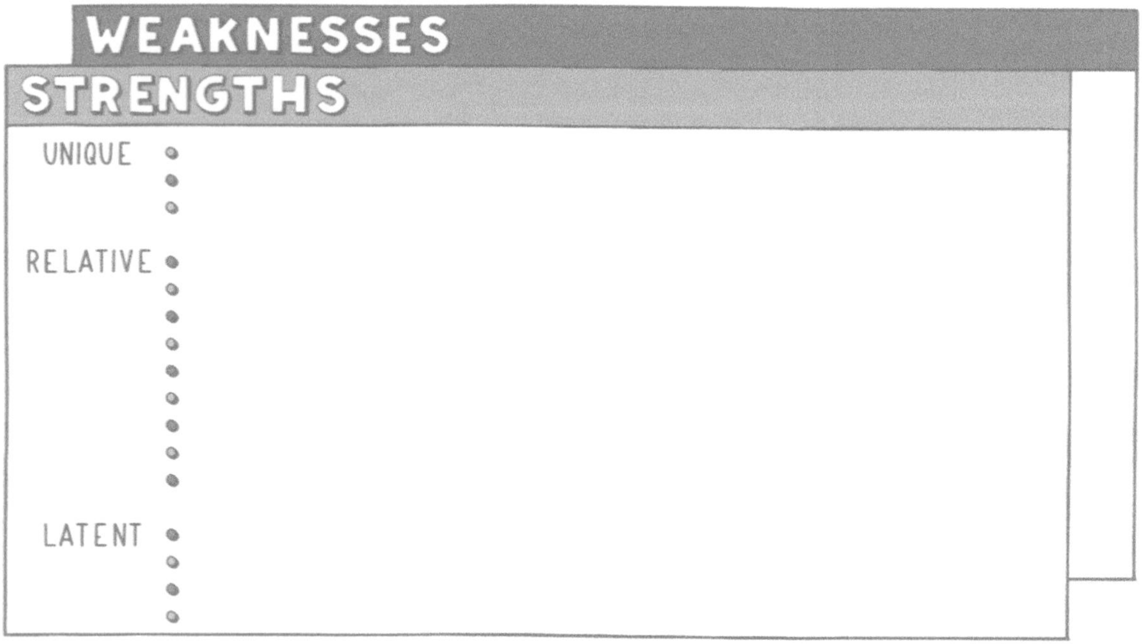

Fig 2.6.1Lc

Latent Strengths

This is the dimension most people struggle with. In my workshops, it is often the hardest one to flush out.

A good metaphor to have in your mind for this one is an iceberg.

Your latent strengths and weaknesses are those that are under the waterline. They're there, but you may not be aware of them. In some circumstances your prospects and customers are more likely to be aware of them. Your customers, suppliers and staff are excellent sources of latent strengths and weaknesses. This valuable insight all too often remains untapped and hidden. You might want to consider sitting down with key stakeholder groups such as customers, suppliers and staff and asking them what they consider to be "less obvious" strengths and weaknesses. This is how you'll start to get clarity of your below the waterline latent strengths and weaknesses.

I once had a client who discovered that their IT system was, in fact, much more agile than their competitors'. This would give them an advantage, but they had no idea about it until they hired a programmer from their biggest competitor. His main motivation for applying for the position was his frustration with the outdated legacy systems at his previous employer.

Top tip: a reminder of how important it is to conduct exit and arrival interviews with staff leaving or joining.

Your senior team might be completely unaware of some latent strength or weakness that your business has, but someone in the warehouse, in customer service, in sales, or in billing knows about it all too well. Establish systems to flush out this incredibly valuable insight.

Another example is a recent client – a mirror making company which discovered a latent strength in their packaging: They have less breakage because their packaging is so good. The senior team might be completely unaware of this. They discovered it during a routine meeting with their logistics supplier who happened to also distribute the mirrors and framed pictures for three of their top competitors. Who knew? They quickly turned this insight into selling points.

So, what I advise companies to do when flushing out this matter of latent strengths, is to hold focus groups with their people, or to do research with their customers, their users and even suppliers. I tell them to go out and observe and see for themselves what is going on.

By talking to the people who really know what's going on, a leadership team can quickly discover their latent strengths and latent weaknesses.

Of course, once you know about the weakness, it shifts over into the dimension of a relative weakness because now you know about it. Now you can start to fix it and remove it altogether so it's no longer a weakness.

Latent Weaknesses

As stated above in Latent Strengths, in addition you might believe that your processes are pretty effective and efficient until you go down to the plant or step into the back office and discover that they aren't.

On closer inspection you might discover underlying:

- Problems
- Blockages
- Inefficiencies

Only by taking a look can you discover these latent weaknesses which, if not handled, could have an enormously detrimental effect on your business and its strategy.

Opportunities and Threats

As mentioned previously, opportunities and threats are generally external.

The essential tasks to perform *before* undertaking your brainstorming are:

- Current profile – success and failures
- Sandbox analysis, your extended marketplace and stakeholder audit

- And your Future Business Arena (FBA) analysis.

These three exercises will help you gain clarity. Clearly, getting visibility of your successes and failures will help you identify some opportunities to improve. Equally, you'll gain visibility of some threats. The sandbox will show you where you are right now in your current trading environment and you can identify all your stakeholders and who the influencers are. The FBA will illuminate what changes you and your team feel are likely to happen during the next three years.

The use of focus groups to understand your latent strengths and weaknesses can also be used here. Those people on the phone lines, handling complaints from customers, are the ones who *really* know where your touchpoints are breaking down and failing to deliver.

Use whatever tools or expertise you have at your disposal to do a thorough current profile, sandbox, Future Business Arena, as well as look at what might be irritating your customers today, in order to have a full picture of the opportunities and threats to your business.

This is a great example of pies or pie charts. Look beyond the pie charts and really get into what your stakeholders think, feel and believe. Open up those pies to find what's inside.

Opportunities

Fig 2.6.3Lc

By definition, these are either right here, right now or in the near or medium term future. Try not to look beyond three years, unless your industry sector requires a greater horizon. They will almost certainly be related to ways you can adapt your company's profile. You'll recall that your profile relates to the products and services that you sell and the customers and users in certain industry sectors or markets and in certain geographical territories who buy.

You should also go beyond *what* you offer to *who* and *where* in your current profile. Also look at *how* you adapt or innovate to take advantage of these opportunities. For example, you could decide to enter new territories through collaboration instead of going it alone, under your own steam.

Once you've formulated your list of opportunities you need to filter them. Some clients we've worked with have included opportunities which "might happen". I usually suggest you park these until they are certain to happen. You've most likely generated a significant list of opportunities that are either here and now or definitely going to happen within a reasonable timeline.

The next thing to consider is the degree of positive impact each opportunity will have on the business if you land it or make it happen. To keep it simple use a low, medium and high (LMH) scale. Then assess the "degree of difficulty" again using an LMH scale. You could go further and allocate a numeric value as well, this could help filter and prioritise if you've got a considerable number of opportunities. Remember though to flip the scale, i.e. high impact = 3 points, but high difficulty = 1 point.

Threats

THREATS	PROBABILITY LOW/MED/HIGH	IMPACT LOW/MED/HIGH
•		
•		
•		
•		
•		
•		
•		

Fig 2.6.4Lc

We all know what threats are. I have just a few pointers to help you maximise this frame. Threats by definition are things that might happen. If they're already happening and damaging your business, then your lack of a suitable rebuttal makes it a "weakness". This should have been picked up in the "weaknesses" frame.

As previously mentioned, it is really important to take a look at the current profile, sandbox and Future Business Arena outputs before attempting to brainstorm your threats. You're looking for shifts in the environment and landscape with specific attention to your stakeholders and influencers. For example – at the time of writing this book there is a real threat facing the hospitality sector in the UK. Many hotels, restaurants and pubs in tourist areas are experiencing soaring energy and wage inflation. Massive food and beverage inflation and a shortage of skilled staff. This is resulting in many businesses offering a reduced menu, shorter opening times and the real and present danger of going out of business.

Once you've completed the brainstorming and have fleshed out all the threats, as with opportunities, we need to filter and prioritise. So the first thing we have to do is assess each one's level of probability. Keep it simple again with the LMH scale. Then we have to assess the impact on the business. I suggest you go again with an LMH scale.

Your plan of action regarding threats is to **reduce their impact** as much as possible, ideally eliminate any negative impact completely. Ask yourself whether you can "flip the script" and even turn a threat into an opportunity? For example:

Around 2010 a serial entrepreneur Tom Allason was making significant inroads in the same day courier market in the UK with Shutl. He'd developed a very smart SAAS platform that enabled omnichannel retailers to pick from stores nearest to the online shopper's delivery address and seamlessly get a courier to collect from a store and deliver, all within 90 mins. This was a potential game changer, a massive disruptor. I identified this as a significant threat to DPD. I met with Tom, turned the threat into an opportunity and convinced Paul-Marie Chavanne, who was then the President of the DPD Group to invest in Shutl. The rest of the board was completely against the investment. Fast forward two years, Ebay bought Shutl for a staggering multiplier of its revenue and DPD got a 10 fold return on its modest initial investment in just over two years. This is one of my favourite examples of turning a threat into an opportunity.

Another obvious example – the single-use plastics ban I talked about earlier in the book has a significant probability of occurring. Companies which count on these single-use plastics to get their product to the user e.g. soft drinks companies, need to plan now for this event. Supermarkets are also looking at ways to reduce plastic packaging, not before time.

Vulnerabilities

Weaknesses and vulnerabilities are not the same thing. Weaknesses as explained earlier in this chapter; whether they're unique, relative or latent, they are about an organisation's capabilities or, to be precise, lack of them. An example I often use to explain this is when a company has a serious dependency on a dated central IT system that it has significantly developed over the years. It's now clunky and becoming restrictive and holding the business back in terms of its innovation capability. This is definitely a "relative weakness" when compared to more agile competitors. Now, the plot thickens. This legacy IT system is solely dependent on a small third party contractor. Every time changes are required the small external contractor is called in to make said changes. What if this contractor goes bust, decides to no longer support your system or the individual with the "know-how" at the supplier retires? This is a vulnerability.

Another example of a vulnerability related to an *individual* could be when you have only one single sales person who has a relationship with a major client. What if this salesperson leaves to join a major competitor? Massive vulnerability.

Vulnerabilities are usually linked to an event or to an individual (who could get ill or have an accident or simply get up and quit).

One final comment on vulnerabilities. When we've conducted one of our critical thinking programmes it always shines a light on some key members of the team or some rising stars who are clearly going to make the difference going forward. In our debrief with the CEO we will always look at how these KPIs (key persons of impact or influence) are being looked after, locked down and their futures secured. I don't necessarily mean this in a contractual "ball & chain" sense, although making sure they're on perhaps a three and six month notice period i.e. they have to give you three months notice and you give them six months, is worth considering. I mean, sit down with them and make sure they know they're appreciated and part of the big picture going forward. Put in place some measures to strengthen the mutual relationship between you and them. Make sure you maintain an engaged and trusting relationship with these stars. Show them the potential for career progression and make it worth their while to stay. In my experience, it's not usually about the money, it's more about feeling fulfilled in their work, appreciated, recognised and showing how they make a valuable contribution to the company's success.

Key Takeaways

SWOT analysis is a simple, well-known and valuable frame to be performed as part of a strategic review or reset. However, it is often done at the wrong time, with minimal information and done poorly as a token box-ticking exercise. Timing and the approach taken is key, a SWOT+ must take place after:

- A full competitive landscape analysis
- A current profile
- A full sandbox analysis
- A full Future Business Arena work-out

Strengths and Weaknesses are generally internal. Opportunities and Threats are usually external.

Strengths and Weaknesses each have three dimensions to them:

- Unique
- Relativity to competitors
- Latency, i.e. under the waterline and perhaps unknown

When working out your opportunities and threats, be sure to think of their probability and impact. Investing significant resources in an opportunity with a low probability is probably not the best use of time and resources.

Vulnerabilities are generally related to a possible *event* or key *person.*

So, there you have it. Easy, when you know when and how.

Get Started

1. Make a quick list of some of your strengths and weaknesses in relation to your competition. This doesn't have to be a thorough workout as this is only possible after completing a comprehensive Competitive Landscape Analysis. The purpose of this exercise is just to get a feel for the action of listing out strengths and weaknesses in relation to your competitors.
2. Make sure to include unique, relative and latent strengths and weaknesses. If you are not sure which latent weaknesses exist, take a walk through your business or set up a focus group and get your peoples' input. When was the last time you conducted exit or arrival interviews with leavers and starters? You might be amazed at what comes up.
3. Similarly, list out some of your opportunities and threats.
4. List out, roughly, what the probability of each of those opportunities and threats is and assess the potential impact i.e. high, medium, low
5. List out the vulnerabilities your business might have as a result of some event, or the loss of some key person associated with your business.

Part 3

Driving Force – The Power of Driving Force

Introduction

This is probably the most important chapter and section in this entire book.

Scan the QR code for this chapter's video

But, like everything else I've touched on so far, the concept of driving force must be understood *in context.*

If your objective is to be a highly successful organisation and deliver sustainable growth, then it can be argued that you will need to have a strategy that delivers a significant and consistent point of relevant differentiation. One that offers either unique value or relative value compared to your competition. If you really want to 'change the game' and 'hold all the cards' then it should be a strategy that others will find impossible or difficult to copy or emulate.

This could be called your "secret sauce" or the defining core of your "business DNA", your *driving force.* It is the component of the business that is at the very heart of your company or organisation. It is the key determinant behind your direction of travel and the management choices made along the way. More than any other strategic area your *driving force* will influence the choices made regarding your products and services, your customers and users, their markets, and geographical areas. Without an understanding of their driving force the senior leadership team (SLT) may have significant challenges regarding their alignment of thinking. In other words, they will almost certainly be split over the direction of travel and where the priorities are. They will also find it almost impossible to create and deliver a growth strategy to beat the competition.

Just as it is impossible to do a meaningful SWOT Analysis in the absence of knowing your competitive landscape, your sandbox and your Future Business Arena, so this crucial section on driving force needs to be seen in *context* with everything that has come before and which will come afterwards in this book.

The concept of driving force will be familiar to well over 3500 organisations globally. These organisations have all successfully deployed the Strategic Thinking process at some point. I, personally, am privileged to have worked with some of the most promising, astute and caring

CEOs and their leadership teams throughout Britain, Europe and beyond. I observed them in 'full flight', trying to finalise their organisations' future growth strategy. Invariably, it develops into a pitch battle between finance and functional SVPs disagreeing about budget levels, timelines, and priorities. The CEO frequently takes on the role of arbitrator and peacemaker. The only common factor shared in the room is a spreadsheet and the EBIT number in the bottom right corner. This is not Strategic Thinking, it is budget planning. No organisation or business can "be the best it can be" unless it understands what is at the very core of their business. What is their 'business DNA', what is their *driving force.*

As a result of the vast experience obtained through working with such a diverse and influential organisation, I have isolated the **only ten component parts or strategic areas** that **every single organisation in the world** is made up of.

Ten Strategic Components

All organisations, whether they are state-owned postal authorities, international conglomerates, SMEs or agile e-commerce startups – they all have 10 strategic components or areas. Without an understanding of their company's driving force, the SLT will have **significant challenges** regarding their alignment of thinking. If the team is not entirely in agreement as to what, precisely, is the company's driving force, they will be *divided* and *split* over the direction of travel going forward. This can be the road to ruin.

Between these areas, leadership must decide where and how to look for opportunities, prioritise their attention and allocate resources. So, what are these 10 strategic components that are present in all organisations?

1. Every company employs ***technology or know-how*** to a greater or lesser extent.
2. Every company makes use of natural ***resources*** to one degree or another.
3. Every company combines these within an operational ***capacity.***
4. This is strengthened to a greater or lesser extent with their in-built ***capability.***
5. All this results in the delivery of consistent ***products or services***.
6. Every company uses a certain mix of ***marketing and sales methods*** to acquire customers.
7. Every company will employ certain ***distribution methods*** to get these products and services to their customers.
8. Every company sells to a certain class of ***customers or end users.***
9. They in turn reside in certain categories or ***market types***.
10. Finally, every company, even not for profit, monitors its ***size, growth, and profit***.

DRIVING FORCE
THE TEN COMPONENTS
TECHNOLOGY/ KNOW-HOW
PRODUCTION CAPACITY
PRODUCT/ SERVICE
SALES & MARKETING METHOD
CUSTOMER/ USER CLASS
SIZE / GROWTH/ PROFIT
NATURAL RESOURCES
PRODUCING CAPABILITY
DISTRIBUTION METHOD
MARKET / TYPE CATEGORY

Fig 3.0c

In practice, one of these will often dominate the Strategic Thinking consistently over time. Favouring or leveraging this one area of the business time and again determines how a leadership team chooses opportunities and allocates resources. Simply put – one of the 10 strategic components is the *de facto* engine room, it is the company's 'DNA', it is their ***driving force***.

To help illustrate this and explore the *driving force* principle further let us examine what each strategic component brings and what it can do to shape a business. I must stress this is very much from the "outside looking in" – I would never tell a company or client what their *driving force* is. Let us look at each strategic area and explore some examples of companies that might select each component as their *driving force*. I must stress that the examples illustrated in this chapter are simply my hypothesis looking from the outside in.

Strategy driven by ***Technology /Know-How***

A technology-driven company is rooted in some basic, hard technology, such as chemistry, physics or soft technology like know-how or expertise. They will excel at being able to commercialise their know-how or technology to drive growth and fund further investment in their know-how/technology. Ideally, they will be able to protect their intellectual property (IP). 3M is probably a technology-driven business. For many years, at the very centre of its business model has been their ability to identify breakthrough technology, buy it, protect the IP and then commercialise it by launching product after product. To date, they have well over 60,000 products. Several years ago, UPS clearly repositioned itself from being a *distribution* driven business to being a *know-how* driven business, obsessing about all things logistics.

Honda is another excellent example of a company that is extremely proficient in a specific technology. In Honda's case, it is the superior tech of their engines. By utilising this technology, Honda is able to consistently produce high-calibre engines for a wide variety of machines such as lawnmowers, motorbikes, marine engines, cars, even jet engines. Finally, in the same sector, look how Tesla have taken their electric vehicle and battery know-how to change the game in the car sector. Tesla is synonymous with EV (electric vehicle) know-how.

Strategy driven by ***Natural Resources***

This covers a company whose entire purpose is centred around the pursuit and exploitation of natural resources. Examples could include oil, gas, gold, lithium, forestry, wind, solar, but also people. Resource-driven businesses will focus significant effort on tracking down new pools of the resource. Equally, they will be experts at converting said resource into a "commercial state" to generate income and growth. Isotrol in Spain has for many years pursued a resource-driven strategy in renewable energy. Many successful recruitment businesses will structure their business around the identification of suitable candidates and then support and coach them to successfully land their dream job. For example, TeamJobs and Select Appointments in the UK do this extremely well. The latter positions itself with the tagline, "Jobs for People and People for Jobs". They are probably a resource-driven business.

PRODUCTION CAPACITY

Strategy driven by Operational ***Capacity***

A company driven by production or operational capacity will almost always have a significant capital entry on their balance sheet. Their entire business depends on the effective utilisation of these assets to generate income. They will often operate 365 days a year and potentially 24/7 if they can. Their strategy is to keep the operation running at or close to capacity continuously. Examples of capacity-driven businesses could include hotel chains, airlines, cruise ships, steel refineries, pulp and paper companies and commercial printers. Many Logistics companies could consider being capacity driven businesses. At the core of their growth strategy could be to sweat their operational network assets 24/7, 365 days a year.

The manager of a large hotel chain might be heard, first-thing on Monday morning, enquiring about the room occupancy, the covers in the restaurant and the takings in the bar over the weekend.

And airlines can't sell a seat once the plane has taken off.

These are all capacity-driven businesses. As mentioned earlier, one of the biggest indicators of a capacity-driven business is that it is capital intensive. The balance sheet is likely to have a significant entry alongside said capital.

PRODUCING CAPABILITY

Strategy driven by Operational ***Capability***

This is when "*capacity* meets *know-how*". In other words, a capacity-driven business recognises that to get an edge over the competition and perhaps change the game they need to invest in some "know-how" to create a sustainable difference. There could be some distinctive capabilities incorporated within its operational process that enable added features to its products that competitors cannot match, at least in the short-term. As a result of this, the company can now either 'fish in a different pond' for its clients or use the newfound capability to secure more business or to command a higher price. In the logistics world we can think of many examples where players have introduced some new software or technology to deliver a relatively enhanced last mile experience. For example, DPD's Predict and Precise services and their app.

Another example could be a printer who invests in a new piece of kit which gives them some significant additional capability such as: security printing, sequential numbering, hologram printing, being able to print on glass or fabric and so on…

PRODUCT/ SERVICE

Strategy driven by ***Product or Service***

A company pursuing a product or service-driven strategy will be obsessive about delighting customers and users through the provision of excellent value for money products or services.

Such companies decide deliberately to limit their strategy to a singular product and its derivatives. As a result, all their future products are genetic extrapolations of the very first product they made – the look, form and function of the product remain constant over time.

Companies driven by product and service achieve growth by offering new products and after-sales service to support the extended range.

Examples of product-driven companies are Coca-Cola (soft drinks), Boeing (aeroplanes), Michelin (tyres), Toyota (cars) and Rolex (watches).

Similarly, a company pursuing a service-driven strategy will "obsess" about delighting customers and users by providing top-of-the-range, value-for-money services. These services tend to revolve around a core service.

Some examples include HSBC (banking), Pukka Insure (insurance), Four Seasons Hotels and Resorts (luxury hospitality).

The last example is a curious one and touches on an important point: just because you're in a specific industry sector, doesn't mean your driving force is automatically selected. Driving force is specific to each business and company. Determining your company's driving force is something that must be done deliberately, taking all factors into account, and only after a *thorough* study of the company's operations and aspirations.

Hotels are usually capacity-driven businesses. In the luxury hospitality industry, capacity is still important, but it is not the driving force behind every strategic move that company makes. The focus of a luxury hospitality business is outstanding service. So, in contrast to a standard hotel manager, the luxury hotel manager doesn't run around on a Monday morning asking about occupancy, restaurant covers and bar takings; they walk around quietly and ensure that every luxury is in place and that Mr and Mrs Important in Suite 405 had their bath salts delivered on time, and with their personal note attached to them.

When I was CMO of the DPD Group in 2011, we were a client of DPI doing a Strategic Thinking Programme at group level for the second time. We changed from distribution to a service-driven business. We'd nailed the operational "coming together and leveraging" that was needed in 2008. In 2011 the focus had to be service excellence. Then in 2017, when DPD invited me back in to run the ST process at group level for the third time, they chose a new and different driving force to take them forward for the next three years.

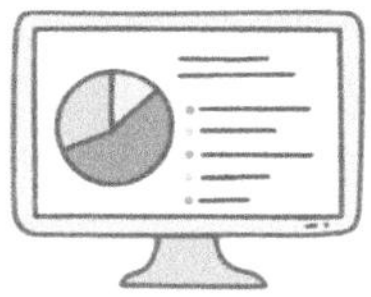

SALES & MARKETING METHOD

Strategy driven by ***Marketing and Sales Method***

Any organisation which harnesses its sales and marketing capabilities to build a business, and makes that the *core* of its DNA, is a business driven by the marketing and sales method.

This company will have a unique or relatively strong marketing and sales platform, process or methodology. They typically sell a wide variety of products through that platform and their growth is driven by introducing more and more products and by increasing the number of customers using their platform. Examples include Ebay, Amazon, Herbalife, QVC and Avon.

These companies invest enormous amounts of focus and effort into fine-tuning the sales experience for both the seller and the shopper.

One of our core principles is that we do not tell companies what their driving force is.

Why am I bringing this up again? Well, let's talk about Amazon.

As an outsider looking in, Amazon looks like a company driven by a sales and marketing method.

But that might be entirely wrong.

Amazon might very well be driven by know-how or capability.

Amazon has led e-commerce *relentlessly* since the very inception of the internet, utilising breakthrough technology from the outset. They were a massive influencer in early cloud technology, launching Amazon Web Services in 2002 before "cloud computing" was even a buzzword.[12] Dropbox piggybacked on this early infrastructure for years before moving onto its own, home-baked solution.[13] So there's a case for Amazon choosing a driving force from several serious contenders.

DISTRIBUTION METHOD

Strategy driven by ***Distribution method***

A company driven by a distribution method will have a unique or relatively strong or distinctive approach to moving tangible or intangible things from one place to another. They do not necessarily have to own the end-to-end system, but they will certainly control or strongly influence it. They achieve growth by focusing on the organisation and expansion of the system or

[12] https://www.computerweekly.com/feature/A-history-of-cloud-computing

[13] https://www.wired.com/2016/03/epic-story-dropboxs-exodus-amazon-cloud-empire/

network. They can also improve their returns by relentlessly seeking to improve its effectiveness. Examples of distribution-driven businesses might include FedEx and many postal authorities.

FedEx, whilst headquartered in Memphis, has a global network of air express hubs connected by one of the largest fleets of cargo planes in the world. In turn, these air hubs connect by regional flights or road-based trunkers to local hubs and depots. Then a final mile fleet of delivery vehicles collect and deliver the last mile. Clearly, FedEx could be a distribution driven business.

BP or Shell's retail network of filling stations could be considered as distribution-driven also. Yet their exploration and green energy divisions could well be considered natural resources and know-how respectively.

Technology platforms such as Netflix, Spotify and Audible could also be considered as *distribution* driven.

CUSTOMER/ USER CLASS

Strategy driven by a ***Customer or User Class***

A company that is driven by a customer or user class has deliberately chosen to restrict its strategy to a describable class of customers or users (people). These customers or users have a 'pulse' and they represent the vast majority of people that the company serves. The company then applies considerable effort to understand the needs, wants and desires of the chosen customer or user class. The company can then grow by continuously looking for fresh ways to satisfy any unmet needs, wants and desires. For example,a shipping software company might decide to become a user class driven business because its best-selling software helps distribution managers in e-commerce and omni-channel retail do their jobs more effectively. They would then obsessively research what else they could sell to these people to make their lives easier. For example, packaging material.

A fictional company called Education Software Limited might decide to become a user class driven business because its best-selling software helps secondary school business managers do their jobs more effectively. They then research what else they could sell to these business managers to make their lives easier.

Some real potential examples of customer or user class businesses include Montblanc (gifts for successful business executives), Johnson & Johnson (they develop products for doctors, nursing professionals, midwives and new mums and dads).

MARKET / TYPE CATEGORY

Strategy driven by ***Market Type***.

A company that is driven by market category has deliberately decided to limit its strategy to a describable marketplace or market type. The core difference between this strategy and "*customer and user class*" is that this is the large grouping of customer/users viewed collectively. For example – e-commerce SMEs.

Let's imagine a hospital. A hospital is composed of nurses, doctors, physiotherapists, radiographers, porters, cleaners, administrators, patients, visitors and many other people with a *pulse*. These individually could be customers or users of your product or service. But the hospital itself is a market type or a market category.

Other examples of market types include:

- Schools
- The Military
- Restaurants
- Couriers

Similar to user class, companies in this category identify everyday needs among the buyers in that market category and then respond with a wide variety of products and services for that market category.

For example, a vending machine company might look at the hospital market category and decide that the *collection of customers* – doctors, nurses, visitors – were interested in healthier products being sold from those machines and so enter into contracts with health food suppliers to deliver it.

These companies often achieve growth by broadening their portfolio of products or by expanding the number of market types. Examples might include Disney which caters to the "wholesome entertainment for the family" market, or Lockheed Martin which caters to the military and in recent years has targeted the logistics space as well.

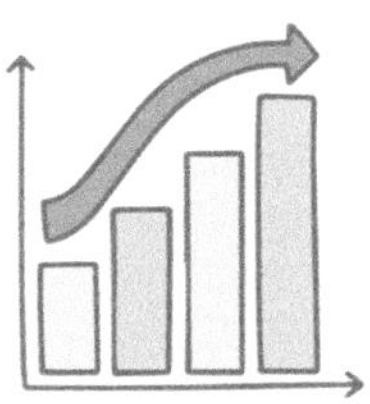

SIZE / GROWTH / PROFIT

Strategy driven by ***Size, Growth and Profit***

A company driven by size, growth and profit tends to be a conglomerate of related or completely unrelated businesses. Its sole focus is to grow a portfolio of business interests. Its expertise is in the leadership and management of this broad range of separate businesses. They will also continuously evolve and improve how they identify target businesses and acquire them. They will often try to standardise the way senior teams within the portfolio do their reporting. Private equity firms may often choose this as their driving force. Other examples could include – Virgin Group, Berkshire Hathaway, GE Capital, Keppel Group.

Virgin Media might be driven by its *Distribution Method.* Virgin Atlantic might choose to be a *"service"* driven business. But Virgin Group, the conglomerate and holding company which controls the Virgin brand, would be driven by *size, growth and profit.*

Conclusion

This is why it is so vital for a company to work out its *own* driving force and not some external consultant.

Deciding on its driving force is probably the most significant single decision a leadership team will take while undergoing our Strategic Thinking Programme. It's so important that the leadership team has a broad and in-depth discussion and explores all the options thoroughly.

In our workshops, we ask the group to reflect on all the insights from previous discussions including sandbox, SWOT+, competition review and especially the Future Business Arena (FBA). We ask them to explore all 10 candidate-driving forces and try to pick the three that could bring the most exciting Future Strategic Profile.

So, what's a Future Strategic Profile (FSP)? The final chapter in Part 3 of the book covers this. Essentially, what products or services you sell, to which customers and users, in which industry sectors and in which geographical territories. Your FSP is exactly the same, but we are conceptualising what we'd like it to be at a certain time in the future. With most clients this tends to be three years in the future. This can be cut shorter if the landscape is particularly fast-moving. Or indeed stretched way beyond three years if the sector is much longer term. For example, the airline industry, shipping industry or large hotel sector where capital expenditure tends to be the largest item on the balance sheet. Therefore the life of the FSP for an airline might be 20 years.

We divide the entire senior team into two or three subteams. Each subteam is given a possible driving force to work with. We invite each subteam to imagine what their business' strategic profile might look like three years from now through the lens of the driving force they were given. It often helps to write it down as if they were three years in the future. For example: "We have transformed our product range to comprise X, Y, Z. Selling over xx,000 units per month to A, B and C customers in O, P, Q industry sectors in Europe, North America and South East Asia. It is critically important that the subteam paints as clear a picture of the exciting Future Strategic Profile that they are committing to build when looking through the lens of the potential *driving force* that team was allocated to explore.

We usually recommend three subteams to develop three alternative Future Strategic Profiles. This however can be restricted to two subteams if the leadership team has fewer than 12 members. They then present the potential Future Strategic Profile back to the entire senior team. This is followed by a discussion amongst the entire team, moderated by myself or whoever is delivering the workshop. We don't move on to the next stage until the whole group is in complete agreement as to what their future driving force is and have signed off on the Future Strategic Profile they're all collectively committing to build.

We never tell a client what their *future driving force* is. It is critically important that the leadership team themselves have a wide and deep discussion to explore all the options thoroughly.

So that is the concept of a *driving force* – "it does what it says on the tin". It is the single most significant strategic area or component that is at the very heart of your business and drives much of your decision making. Until now, this was something the senior team might have been doing subconsciously. By understanding the power of the driving *force* and transferring it to a deliberate cornerstone of your strategic approach it can then become a game changer. Once you decide what your *driving force* is and what it should be during the next 3 years or so, it will unlock whole new levels of critical thinking.

Key Takeaways

Your company's driving force sits at the very heart of the business, it's your core DNA.

Every company is active in all ten strategic areas to some extent or other. But only one of those areas runs through the core of the organisation – that area is the one that *drives* the company forward.

Once you and the rest of the SLT have selected the driving force and agreed on the Future Strategic Profile, decisions suddenly become more aligned and easier to make.

Allocating resources and priorities is also so much easier.

Action Steps

1. Think of some brands or companies you're familiar with and consider what their driving force might be.
2. What is the driving force of your business, company, or organisation today? (Tip: try starting by eliminating the components that definitely aren't your current driving force.)
3. How does that inform your decision making, priorities and allocation of resources?
4. Now considering the Future Business Arena and SWOT+, which two alternative driving forces could bring an exciting new impetus to your business?
5. If you adopted either of these, how would that impact on your decision making, focus and resource allocation for the other one? Is it possible to invoke a combination of them to describe your ethos or 'business DNA'?

Remember, as always, keep your thinking pure and simple.

KNOWING YOUR
DRIVING FORCE
GIVES YOU
AN EDGE.

Driving Force – The Power of Knowing

One of the questions I get asked consistently while delivering the Strategic Thinking Programme is, "Well, if you're a printer or a hotel, won't your driving force automatically always be capacity?" Or, more specifically worded: "Well, aren't *all* businesses in that industry capacity-driven?"

I touched on this briefly in the previous chapter with the Four Seasons Hotel, but let's delve deeper into it because it's an important topic to know thoroughly, and there are nuances to it that must be understood fully.

Scan the QR code for this chapter's video

As you saw quite clearly in the previous chapter, the answer to the above question is a definite no. One business in a particular industry sector does not automatically fall into the same driving force category as another.

That's why going through this exercise during the Strategic Thinking Programme is so vital.

But there's another thing: k*nowing* what your driving force is, and knowing it to your core, gives you an edge like no other over any competitors who don't know, consciously, what their driving force is.

"Knowing your driving force gives you an edge."

Exploiting it with your ***areas of excellence*** makes you deliver on that edge (more about this in the next chapter).

Let's look at another example of two companies in the same industry, yet who have a completely different driving force.

Michelin makes exceptional tyres. They're probably a *product-driven* business. (Remember, an outsider looking in). They have a few other fringe products, but, without any doubt, their main revenue driver is tyres. Perfecting this core product and consistently delivering a great product would suggest to me that they're currently probably a Product-driven business.

At first glance, you might think Continental was also a product-driven business producing exceptional tyres also. But if you visit their website, you'll notice that it's *all* about innovation.

From my perspective as an outsider looking in, they are a *Know-How driven* business. They have exceptional know-how in safety systems, brake systems, drive systems, tyre technology etc.

In the next chapter I show you how you can truly leverage your driving force to change the momentum of your business and change the game. I'll share how each driving force has two or three ***areas of excellence***. By simply being outstanding at these you will outperform your competitors, whether they have the same driving force or not.

Changing Your Driving Force

It's not just about *understanding* your driving force.

Once you know your driving force, you have the power to change it in order to change the fortunes of your business within the changing Future Business Arena you'll be operating in.

We've talked about the following two examples before, albeit in reference to other sections: 3M and Montblanc. (Incidentally, if you can get hold of a copy of "The new Strategic Thinking, pure & simple by Mike Robert published by McGraw Hill you'll read about how 3M used DPI's services many times to shape its strategy over many years)

3M was a product-driven business thirty years ago. They produced tape: duct tape, masking tape, etc.

Then they changed their driving force and became a technology and know-how driven business. They scoured the planet for exceptional, groundbreaking technology, bought the patents, and then commercialised them. This is what they are truly exceptional at.

They now have over 60,000 products.

I shared my thoughts with you regarding Montblanc in the sandbox section. Just as they changed their sandbox, so did they adopt a new driving force – from product-driven to user-class-driven. They started producing gifts for successful business executives. They became a user-class-driven business. Whereas they made only pens before, they were now producing cufflinks, belts, document holders, briefcases, sunglasses, perfumes, watches, briefcases, phone cases, aftershaves, etc.

By changing their driving force, they completely transformed their business. They're competing in a much bigger market with a completely different approach to sales and marketing. If you fly via an international airport, you can pretty much guarantee you'll see a Montblanc store in the departure area.

Another example – McDonald's is probably a capacity-driven business. You don't want to stay long because the chairs are a little uncomfortable and the lighting is too bright. The seating doesn't encourage you to sit around there and wait for hours. It's fast food, fast eating, fast turnover of customers. The first question the manager or franchisee will ask about the previous day is likely to be volume and revenue based.

Here's a hypothetical example:

There are more and more coffee shops on the high street. Practically on every high street in the UK, you will find a Starbucks, a Nero and a Costa Coffee. You'll find independent coffee shops there as well.

In 2000, you'd find two coffee shops per high street. Now there are ten.

My perspective (outsider looking in) is that these coffee shops are capacity-driven businesses. Their business model is to attract passing take-out trade and to have as many people and tables as possible shoved into the coffee shop, have the people sit, have their coffee and food, then leave so the server can come and wipe the table down for the next group of people to come in and sit down.

They're capacity-driven businesses. They each try to "out barista" the other. They focus on the unique or relatively better roast of coffee bean etc. etc. All very vanilla and subjective.

Now, let's imagine one of these coffee shops decided to change their driving force to a user-class-driven ***model.***

User-class-driven businesses target one or a few specific, describable customers or user groups.

Imagine one of these coffee shops decided to target, say, "busy business people who wanted to have meetings face-to-face". These business people could be salespeople or consultants who wanted to meet their clients for a coffee.

In addition to business people, the coffee shop also decides that they're going to target, say, "parents with young children".

After researching what these two distinctive customer groups need and want they may decide to change the layout of their coffee shop:

- Upstairs, they could have a business lounge that can only be accessed by an individual membership card which costs them £99 a month. The card gives the business person access to the lounge, a free coffee, unlimited WiFi inside the lounge and perhaps table service. The lounge would probably be tranquil, with no music playing. The seating might be in cubicles with soundproofing screens up on all sides so that they could have conversations about business without being interrupted or sharing all the business secrets with eavesdroppers.
- This coffee shop could integrate a business lounge into their design which could be booked online for a certain fee. Payment for drinks and meals might be done via direct debit so you can just get up and go afterwards.
- The whole feel of it would be like an airport business lounge.
- But downstairs, for the mums or dads, would be entirely different. There would be high chairs and a play area, a nappy changing unit with free nappies, a magician on Thursdays to entertain the kids.

If you were a business professional, where would you go for a coffee? Nero? Of course not! You'd go to this new place that catered to every one of your needs. Same for the mums. Take the kids to the Costa? Goodness, no! Mum and Dad need a break, the kids are playing safely with new friends in the soft play area and they're tucking into a well-deserved creamy coffee that costs twice as much. It ticks so many boxes.

That's an example of how any of these coffee shops on the High Street could change their driving force, think differently and create a compelling business proposition that changes the way the game is played. Let the other vanilla coffee shops scrap over barista baloney.

This book follows the precise sequence of our Strategic Thinking Programme and choosing to change your driving force is something that mustn't be done lightly. Ideally you have completed all the previous stages of the ST programme.

Once you've successfully established your current profile, sandbox, competitor audit, , worked out your Future Businesses Arena, done your SWOT+, *then* you can start considering changes to your driving force.

By going through the earlier steps, you know what your current model looks like, and you know what your Future Business Arena looks like. You know what your relative strengths and weaknesses are. You've identified potential vulnerabilities. You've assessed the probability and impact of threats and opportunities.

At *that* stage, you can take a good, hard look at your driving force, and consider what your driving force *could* be in order to really springboard some significant and sustainable growth as a result of thinking in a structured way.

That's the power of driving force and what it's all about.

Once you've discovered your company's driving force and fully understand it, you are then in a position to be able to ask yourself this fundamental question:

> *"What should our driving force be in the future in order to maximise the opportunity for growth for our business?"*

Key Takeaways

The power of knowing your driving force cannot be underestimated.

By knowing your driving force, you are then able to change it, if it makes good strategic sense to do so.

To be able to do this thoroughly, so as to maximise the effectiveness of your strategy, you must go through all earlier steps covered in this book.

If you successfully change your driving force, you can really springboard your company's growth.

Action Steps

1. Work out, hypothetically, what a different driving force for your company could be.
2. Like the coffee shop that changed from capacity-driven to customer/user class driven, choose one left of field driving force and imagine how that could completely reshape your proposition and positioning.

Driving Force – Areas of Excellence

Once you've discovered your future driving force, how do you unlock it?

How do you unleash the real power behind that decision to drive your business forward?

A critical concept behind the driving force is the principle of areas of excellence.

Scan the QR code for this chapter's video

The good news is that, for each driving force, there are only **two** or **three** areas of excellence that you need to master in order to excel at making your chosen driving force the key to your business' success.

The other good news is that we've discovered and codified precisely what these areas of excellence are for each driving force.

No matter what driving force you have settled on as the future propelling power within your business, all you need to do now is master the respective areas of excellence for that driving force in order to make your competitive power almost unstoppable.

I'm going to take each driving force in turn and explain the areas of excellence appropriate for each one. There are two or three areas you have to be *genuinely fantastic* at in order to become the game changer you want to be.

Technology or Know-How

1. Research

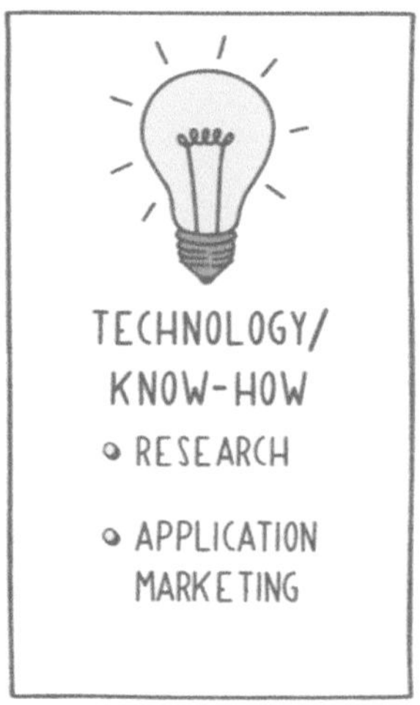

A company that is technology or know-how driven uses technology or know-how as its edge. In a technology or know-how driven business, you have to *continually* seek new ways to sustain that edge. These companies must excel at researching and maintaining their cutting-edge in that particular technology or know-how. Sony famously used to spend 10% of its turnover on research, three times the levels of its main competitors. Peer2peer is a know-how driven business and, as such, we are always reviewing the latest thinking and refreshing our frames to ensure we maintain leading edge thinking within our programmes to help clients with their critical thinking to build amazing teams and businesses. I am aware of many business coaching franchises that have not fundamentally refreshed their material in over 20 years. They've shifted their driving force away from know-how to distribution. It's all about growing and organising their global network of licenced coaches and effectively managing and getting their fee income from their franchisees. A good example of this is Action Coach whose entire business model is driven towards finding and hanging on to coaches. Coaches represent the most lucrative element of their business model. Hence, they may have started as a know-how driven business but are now probably a distribution driven business.

Let's imagine you're a social media trainer, you're quite possibly a know-how driven business. Other companies pay you to guide them in navigating and leveraging social media platforms in order to help scale their businesses. Clearly, researching and understanding how LinkedIn, Instagram, Facebook, Pinterest, TikTok, X etc. change their algorithms or functionality and how the best players engage with their marketplace. If you're quicker at translating platform changes into beneficial training for your clients, you'll quickly gain momentum over your competitors. You will also turn your activities into social media 'science', evaluating client campaigns, refining targeting, adopting new platforms and ways to outperform the competition. It's a constantly changing and developing marketplace and the best social media management companies have to be at the top of their game on the latest developments. They will almost certainly be know-how driven businesses and must be outstanding at research in order to maintain excellence in this area.

2. Application Marketing

Application marketing is *vital.*

How does the technology-driven company make money *using* that technology or know-how? How does one take that tech and know-how *to market*?

These companies must work out ways to create a real desire for their tech and their products. They must be very proficient at identifying commercial applications for said technology or know-how.

3M is, again, another great example to look at when considering know-how or technology-driven businesses. 3M excels tremendously in the area of exploring and then identifying *others* who have a particular IP and then buying that IP and integrating it into their business. This is the *research* area of excellence.

Whether that know-how is software, a chemical formula or some other unique IP, 3M is an expert at locating it and then commercialising it. Their know-how is in commercialising. This is the *application marketing* area of excellence.

As an example, you're a software developer and you've just developed a cool app that brings together in one place all the elements that mobile tradespeople may need. It's got a booking, billing, feedback, even a loyalty scheme. Now what? This is where application marketing comes into its own. How can we adapt this app to earn money? Let's brand it and aim it specifically at self-employed tradespeople – plumbers, hairdressers, etc. We could then partner with one of the cloud accounting software providers such as Xero or QuickBooks, then have the app automatically scan receipts into these cloud accounting tools.

Back to the social media trainer. So they've built processes and systems to keep on top of social platform changes. How can they monetise this know-how? Let's set up a "Social Club", produce a load of video content and get it onto Kajabi. Companies can send employees on social selling courses. We could run boot camps over Zoom, run LinkedIn live training taster sessions etc. etc.

If you're a know-how or technology-driven business you have got to excel at both keeping in front of everybody else by being outstanding at research and then translating your technology or know-how into revenue streams – application marketing.

Attributes and growth

One of the attributes of companies in this category is that they must create a conveyor belt of a perpetual pipeline of innovation in order to stay ahead of the competition.

Growing or scaling a technology or know-how driven business is done by:

- Continuously researching to improve and evolve the tech and know-how you have, as much as developing new ones.
- Either developing it yourselves in-house or finding it elsewhere and securing the rights or licence for it.
- Finding new and exciting applications for the tech and know-how to generate new or stronger revenue streams.
- Build a reputation for this, so that ultimately startups and innovators in your space gravitate to you.

Natural Resources

1. Exploration

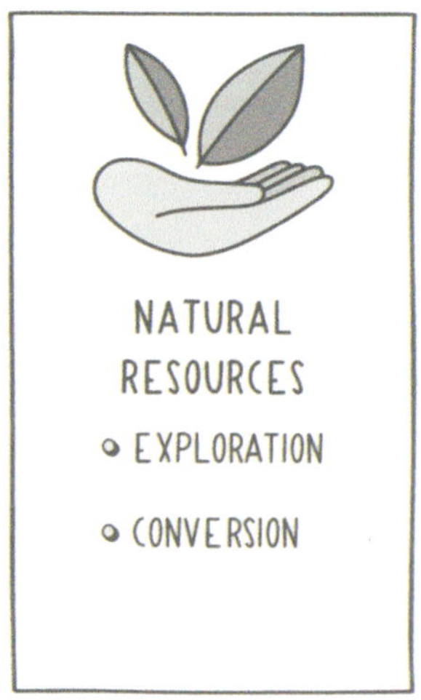

To succeed as a natural resources business, you must be able to **find** the natural resource, e.g. through exploration.

Let's start with a very simple example. The drive towards greener transport has seen a massive surge in EVs (electric vehicles). The current technology in the batteries is underpinned by lithium. Subsequently the market for lithium has rocketed. At the time of writing this book Australia supplies around 60% of the world's lithium. However, Chile has by far the largest lithium reserves estimated at 9.2 million tons (Source statita.com). Clearly, there is a massive opportunity for companies to be at the forefront of the "lithium rush".

No matter what the resource is, companies in this category *must explore* and *find* that natural resource. Being *excellent* at finding and securing the commercial rights is going to be a game changer. Reuters announced in December 2020 that China's Sichuan Yahua Industrial Group Co Ltd had secured a five-year deal to supply Tesla Inc with lithium hydroxide for their batteries.

If you're a recruitment consultancy or platform like Monster or Indeed.com, your entire business model hinges on you finding and attracting quality candidates. By finding the right people to fit your clients' needs is at the heart of being successful or not. This has never been more significant than right now. In the UK, as an example, in some sectors there are way more vacancies than candidates. This phenomenon is set to continue, making the identifying and representing of candidates DEFCON 1 critical.

However, having the candidates or the lithium or the mineral water is only half the battle. Converting it into an accessible commodity to be sold as effectively as possible is the next challenge.

2. Conversion

Effective and efficient conversion of that resource into money by making it into a commodity that can be sold at an optimum price is essential.

Let's develop the example of the recruitment consultancy or platform a little further. If they can excel at finding and signing up good candidates then the next critical step is to match them with a vacant temp or permanent position and to help them land it. They might choose to excel in adding value to their resources by:

- Training them in specific fields and fine-tuning their interview technique.
- Tweaking their CVs so they look more impressive.
- Undertaking a personality profile to help the candidate to understand what puts them in "flow" – I recommend Contribution Compass.
- Give them a useful briefing about the company's background and culture.

Companies driven by natural resources must be able to take this "raw" resource and convert it into something that can be taken to market. Excelling at doing this better than anyone else will set your business apart.

Conversion is the second area of excellence.

Attributes and growth

One of the attributes of companies in this category is that they must *own or control* that resource, in a sense. If the resource is gold, they must own or have a licence for the land and mines in which the gold is mined. If the resource is a person, they must get them to sign some sort of representation deal, preferably exclusive.

Growing or scaling a resource-driven business is achieved by:

- Establishing a significantly better way of discovering or finding the resource.
- Ensuring you're better at the development or conversion of that resource.
- You effectively build a reputation for both previous points.

Strategy Driven by Production Capacity

1. Manufacturing or Operational Efficiency

Efficiency and effectiveness are not the same things. You could have a lawnmower engine that works really efficiently, but the power isn't transferred *effectively* to the underlying blades and so it doesn't mow the grass.

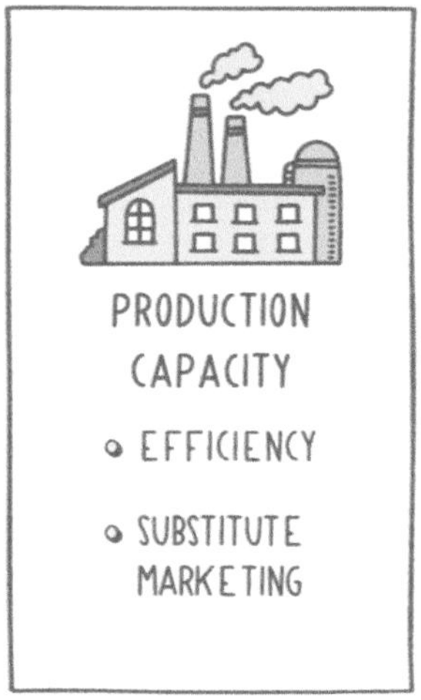

A capacity-driven business must excel at both operational efficiency and effectiveness. They go hand in hand.

Most hotels, restaurants and airlines are capacity-driven businesses.

One of the clues to determine if a business is capacity-driven is that the business has a capital-intensive business model. The biggest item on their balance sheets is the capital assets which are core to the business – the hotel, the aeroplanes, the restaurant's premises, a railway line and the trains. If you run a haulage business this would be your lorries, your depots and your hubs.

Every time these companies buy more assets they increase or maintain their capacity. The essence of these businesses is to "sweat that asset" and absorb the additional step cost increase as quickly as possible so that their EBIT (Earnings Before Interest and Tax) doesn't take a hit. Indeed, many capacity-driven businesses will measure EBIT rather than EBITDA which shows the EBIT after depreciation and amortisation of those assets.

If a parcel company decides to open a new hub it needs that hub teeming with parcels from *day one* of them switching the lights on – ideally.

These companies work on a step cost model. That hub has to be filled as quickly as possible. That hotel has to hit the magic xx% occupancy level pronto, that new Airbus has to be full of premium paying passengers before its maiden flight. There's a critical mass, a tipping point when the company can start making money from that asset.

To survive (and thrive) as a capacity-driven business, these companies must be extremely efficient at scaling their capacity and then filling it through effective marketing.

The second area of excellence for a capacity-driven business is substitution marketing

2. Substitution Marketing

Substitution Marketing is how a business sub-divides its assets in order to cater for different client or customer needs or wants. By excelling at substitution marketing they will identify and implement new applications to make use of the capacity. Capacity-driven businesses usually strive to have the assets generating revenue 24/7/365. The easiest way to explain exactly what substitution marketing is would be to illustrate some examples.

When an airline invests in a number of long-haul intercontinental planes, it won't necessarily segment the cabin in the same way across its newly acquired fleet. For flights between say Madrid and Buenos Aires it might divide the space as follows: 5% first class, 10% business and 85% economy. However, for its London to New York leg it might be 15% first class, 25% business class, 10% premium economy and 50% economy. They base it on the predicted passenger profile needs and wants.

Similarly, many large hotel chains will adapt the room mix depending on the location and predicted demand. In other words, they optimise the potential revenue through a mix of double, twin, family rooms, junior suites and suites.

Attributes and growth

One of the attributes of capacity-driven businesses is that they have a significant focus on investing in capital to create more and more capacity to grow. They're also extremely focussed on improving efficiency and, wherever possible, reducing costs through scale advantages.

Growing or scaling a capacity-driven business is achieved by:

- Sweating those assets 24/7, every day of the year.
- Optimising the revenue by generating exciting new value-adds, making the capacity work better for you.

Strategy Driven by Capability

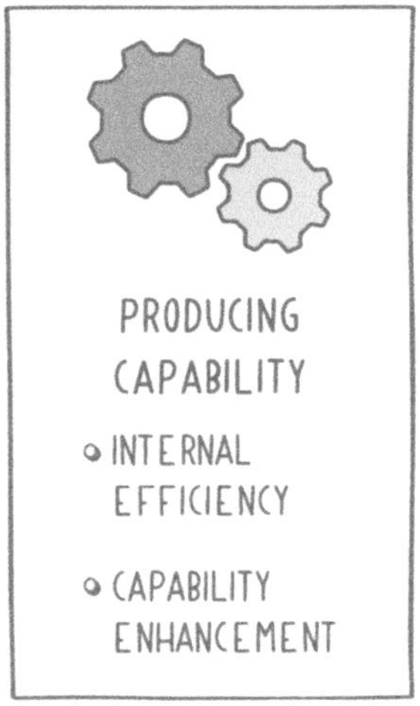

Simply put, a capability-driven business is when a capacity-driven business adds some technology or know-how to differentiate itself from the competition. Capability can be manufacturing capability, technological capability, operational capability, production capability or any other capability that your company can be relatively better at delivering than your competition. Clearly, try to choose a capability that is attractive and appealing to customers. An additional capability that gives you an edge and customers are willing to pay extra for. In my experience customers will pay a little more for a significant additional benefit.

YOU HAVE THE POWER TO CHANGE YOUR DRIVING FORCE IN ORDER TO ADAPT TO THE FUTURE BUSINESS ARENA.

1. Internal Efficiency

These companies need to be extremely efficient at what they do. They can't afford to waste time or to have unnecessary repetition. They need to be constantly reviewing back-office systems, production and processes that drive their operations and delivery of their proposition. They need to modify their tech so that they can do more, and do it better.

In order to be a capability-driven business you'll need to relentlessly review the efficiency and effectiveness of your systems and processes. Try looking at parallel industries that have similar dynamics to your own and see how they operate. What do they do? What tech do they deploy and how? Also consider taking a look at the same industry but non-competing players. For example, they compete in other geographical territories.

2. Capability Enhancement

These companies need to continually improve what they do. Instead of focusing solely on how much they can get out the door, they need to focus on how much they can *improve* a product and deliver something that has the edge over what their competitors are doing.

More often than not, a capability-driven business was previously probably a *capacity-driven* one. Capacity-driven businesses work on a scale game. With greater capacity, a company can usually drive its unit costs down. But not every company has the deepest pockets, and so they realise that they need to compete on a level of *capability* as opposed to capacity.

They then did some serious Strategic Thinking and determined that in order to stand out from their capacity-driven competitors they needed something special, some know-how or specialist expertise that would be the secret sauce for growth. By bolting this know-how or technology onto their core fundamental of being capacity-driven, they morphed into a capability-driven business.

Building in that capability then gives the company the advantage they didn't previously have. A capacity-driven hotel might decide one day to bring in an outstanding chef who produces the most exquisite, exotic food. This would give them an enhanced menu. They could have differently themed food nights. They've built a capability that its competitors can't match, at least for the short term. At least one competitor will soon copy your success formula.

A gym might enhance its capability by having an excellent physical instructor on board who specialises in, say, helping business people relax. Maybe they run meditation sessions on certain mornings or evenings. They could perhaps install video and AV equipment to enable them to launch a Youtube live channel… You get the picture.

Attributes and growth

Capability enhancement is all about bringing additional complementary know-how, a particular skill or capability into your business. Keep adding and modifying your capability, then your competitors will be on continuous catch up. This then allows you to offer products or services of a different (or higher) quality, and perhaps even enables you to charge a premium on these products or services. At the very least, people will see that they get better value for their money from you than from your competitors because you have that additional capability.

Growth will come through a buoyant product innovation pipeline resulting from your newfound capability.

That's why these companies must excel tremendously in the area of capability enhancement.

Strategy Driven by Product and Service

1. Product Development

A real product-driven business will have 90% or so of its revenue coming from a product or range of products containing similar core features.

As a crude example, Toyota makes most of its money on products which contain an engine, a drive train, wheels and seats. You wouldn't expect Toyota to suddenly go develop and sell baby formula.

If you hear the word Rolex, what's the next product you expect to come out of their factory? Would it be a watch or a child's playhouse? It doesn't matter if they decide to launch a James Bond 60th anniversary special edition watch or a watch commemorating the Tour de France's 120th anniversary – you expect a watch from them.

The number one critical focus of a product-driven business is to produce consistent products well and meet the minimum expectation purchasers have every single time. You need an effective new product development system. You need to be outstanding at it.

The same applies to service. If you are a service-driven business, you are determined to deliver a *consistent* level of service that is absolutely predictable. It doesn't necessarily mean it's a premium service. It must merely be a predictable service which the customer is happy to pay for. Critically you and your team will be obsessively focussed on delivering the expected services every single time.

We have often worked with clients who entered a Strategic Thinking process as a capacity or distribution-driven business, but left it with a desire and a blueprint to become a service-driven business. Becoming outstanding at product development or service delivery means they must have a regular process for understanding what their customers' needs, wants and desires are. This requires having clear insight which feeds into the R&D which drives new product development or service delivery.

They don't need to develop entirely new services, but simply add "touches" or improvements or modifications to their *core* service. Toyota must consistently create new vehicles that delight their tribe.

2. Sales and Service

Additionally, companies specialising in products and services need to be able to *sell that product or service*. They will invest significantly in efficient and effective sales approaches. They'll produce very effective sales and marketing collateral. They'll deploy outstanding CRM systems and processes. Sales reward systems will be clear and well understood. In a nutshell, a product and service driven business will be forever fine-tuning and improving its sales processes and performance. It will be obsessive about being better at it than its competitors.

They also need to offer excellent after-sales service, which is appropriate for the company's price point.

During the writing of this book, my Macbook Pro broke. I took it into the store, was massively frustrated. The Mac Team was amazing. They immediately empathised and reassured me that they could retrieve everything and have me back up and running within the hour. Even though the laptop broke within three months of purchase, the service was excellent, they fixed it promptly and I'm still a big fan of Apple.

It's a well-worn expression in business – things will go wrong from time to time, a product fails or the service dips, but it's how you deal with the resulting issues. That's what after sales service is about.

The second area of excellence can be split into a second and third. Some clients see this as being so critical they choose to reinforce their determination to be world class. They focus on sales and service separately.

Attributes and growth

A product and/or service driven business needs to own, define and control the characteristics of its products /service. The products differ but don't fundamentally change. The form and function of the product will not change either.

As we've discussed previously, growth comes through modifications, extensions and adaptations of the product range, outstanding sales and after sales service.

Strategy Driven by Marketing and Sales Method

These companies have a system, a platform or a process that is geared to getting people to buy something from them.

Examples of these companies are Amazon, eBay, QVC and Herbalife.

1. Sales Recruitment

SALES & MARKETING METHOD

- SALES RECRUITMENT
- SELLING EFFECTIVENESS
- EFFECTIVE MANAGEMENT INFO

In sales recruitment, we are referring to the "recruitment" of *products to sell*, not the hiring of salespeople.

The giveaway which determines whether businesses are in this category is that they have a tremendously large variety of products for sale which are often entirely unrelated, and not necessarily produced by themselves.

Amazon and eBay could sell anything if they wanted to. And, indeed, their business model is partly built around the fact that virtually anybody can upload a product and sell it using their platform.

A marketing and sales method business must try to be the best it can possibly be at attracting clients to sell their products through their channel e.g. QVC, a network e.g. Avon or a platform e.g. eBay. They should be looking to recruit new clients as effectively as possible and making the on-boarding process slick and painless.

Another more recent example of sales recruitment is digital sales funnels. By their nature they're built on very effective platforms with the primary purpose to pull prospects along a journey, often starting with a free offer and culminating in them buying a full offer further down the funnel.

The prime question is, "what else can we push through that sales channel to make money?" In a hypothetical example, Avon could have a look at its main buyers and discover that a large proportion of them are mums. Avon could then decide to sell an entirely different product along with its makeup, targeted specifically at mums, such as weekend breaks or anything else which that sales channel and method could handle. They could partner with companies that provide those products.

2. Selling Effectiveness

The buying experience must be fantastic. These companies need to excel at delivering a shopping experience to the user which is unmatched and makes them want to buy more. Repeat business is the key; make it so good customers will come back again and again.

Amazon tracks your history, it knows what you've looked at and purchased before, so it can make intelligent recommendations about what else you might be interested in. When you look at a product, you get comparisons, user reviews. After purchasing the product, the return service is easy to understand and use, and often painless to go through. The advent of cookies also allows them to do some 'social stalking' ads that remind you of products you've looked at but not bought.

eBay is the same – they excel on the *effectiveness* of the sale.

This even goes down to advanced data analysis tools which study buyer trends on their website and accumulate data in order to determine which products and pages work better than others so as to improve those that are lacking. (This last point touches on the final area of excellence: effectiveness of information management systems.

The *effectiveness* of the sale is an area of excellence, regardless of whether the business is online or offline.

More traditional businesses like Amway and Herbalife are so-called network marketing businesses which have, likewise, honed their sales *effectiveness* to a fine degree. All the products are delivered to the salesperson; they come round for a visit, arrange small house parties and engage in networking – sales *effectiveness*.

3. Effectiveness of Information Management System

Even before the internet and data systems, the information management systems of these companies have always been top-of-the-game.

These companies need to know:

- What has sold the best?
- Where has it sold the best?
- What markets buy more?
- Which salespeople sell the most?
- What geographical areas buy the most?
- And a plethora of other metrics that they must track in order to improve their sales method.

Today, this has reached almost science fiction levels of sophistication as peoples' purchasing history and browsing habits are tracked, logged and then analysed by these companies or their marketing divisions.

I have no doubt that QVC keeps track of data that tells them when precisely people switch their TVs on or off, which infomercials have a higher retention rate, which products or presenters make people flip the channel and at what times of the day people are more glued to their TV.

In the past, such information was aggregated and, for lack of a better word, mostly guessed at. TV ratings of hit shows by BARB used to be aggregated from just 5,000 households (and maybe still are), so the figures of programmes that used to have '20 million viewers' were just guesswork.

Today, following the arrival of digitally-delivered TV, knowing these things is a matter of course.

Attributes and growth

The platform or network or channel needs to have a simple and effective means to secure the orders. If they want to scale, they need to delimit the products that can be sold. Finally, they need to have an agnostic open system that can sell any goods or services.

Growth comes through growing your range of products sold and your customers or markets that are buying – pure and simple.

Strategy Driven by Distribution Method

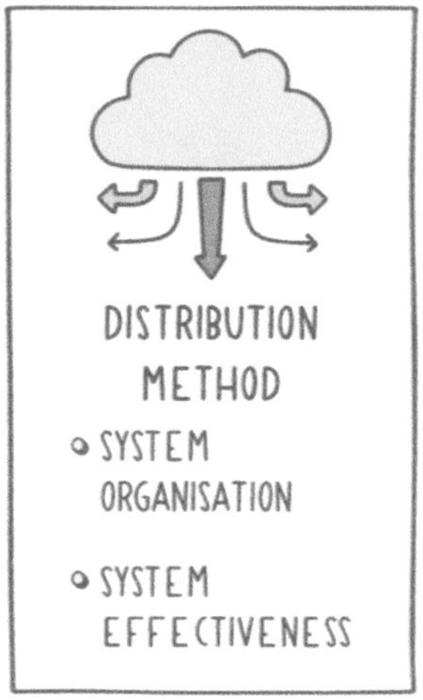

1. System Organisation

If your driving force is distribution, then you have to excel at system organisation and system effectiveness. In a previous chapter I talked about FedEx being a possible example of an excellent distribution-driven business. They specialise in having an infrastructure that will move documents, parcels or pallets from point A to point B through their system. In order to win in their business arena they have to organise their network extremely well. Whether they choose to own, JV, licence, partner or have strategic alliances, they must organise for the effective flow of both physical items and the parallel data and information flows. And they must do it as *effectively* as possible.

BP filling stations could be considered a distribution method driven business. It's all about where they locate their branches – outside city centres or on the main roads where people are driving in or out of city areas. How they move fuel and retail goods through the supply chain to this retail network.

Whilst there is a strong probability that a number of competitors will also be distribution-driven, whoever deploys the smartest, most adaptable and agile organisation will win out.

2. System Effectiveness

Having the smartest, most agile and adaptable organisation is only half the story. The leadership team must also be outstanding at relentlessly fine-tuning and perfecting organisation effectiveness. Ensuring all the parts work as effectively as possible, delivering optimum performance all the time is the ultimate goal.

7-Eleven, FedEx, BP – these are all businesses that have to have very clear and strong strategies around the way they *organise* the network and the *effectiveness* of the supply chain feeding the network.

"THINKING IS
THE HARDEST
WORK THERE IS.
WHICH IS
PROBABLY THE
REASON SO FEW
ENGAGE IN IT."
-HENRY FORD

Attributes and Growth

When we work with clients who have selected distribution as their future driving force, they will mobilise two teams to specifically focus on delivering an ambitious critical issue project for both system organisation and system effectiveness. It's this critical focus that makes the difference.

In order to flourish, they must own or control a distribution network that is relatively stronger than the competition. Then they must leverage this strength by broadening the customers and markets that use their network.

Strategy Driven by Customer or User Class

1. Market Research

An important reminder of terms: a customer or user is a *person*. It is an individual with a pulse. It's a describable individual(s). Often the customer and user are the same person, but sometimes they're not. The customer pays the bill and the user uses the product or service.

It is impossible to be an effective customer-driven business without knowing what your customer and user desires, needs and wants are. It's vital that a consumer/user class driven business deploys a significant amount of effort, focus and ample resources behind truly understanding these identified customers/users.

Remember the Montblanc example. They went from only selling pens to selling products aimed at a specific customer or user type: premium gifts for business executives.

The starting point is usually identifying that a significant number of customers fall into a single or few very distinctive describable groups. For example, you could be a SAAS business. You realise that school business managers represent 20% of your sales. You'd then dig a little further and undertake significant research to truly understand the "pain" that needs fixing. Fast forward six months and you've developed extensions to your product specifically for this attractive customer group. The solution now also:

- Helps staff rostering
- Has a project management solution for premises jobs
- Coordinates delivery book-ins for suppliers
- Allows after-hours bookings for school facilities
- Has a series of templates to help manage school processes inc trips, onboarding staff etc.

You get the picture.

Remember the earlier example of a café that splits its footprint into a section for parents with young children and a section upstairs dedicated to business people. In this case, they're still a café serving anybody, but, they're specifically focusing on two very describable customer groups.

2. Customer Loyalty

Once you've got a clear strategy to focus on a specific customer(s)/user(s) you have to be excellent at building strong loyalty from them. Successful customer/user driven businesses will have a detailed, highly effective programme to capture, retain and grow deep relationships with their target prospects.

If you're a parent you'll know that when you left the hospital for the first time with your baby you will almost certainly have had a bag full of newborn baby stuff like nappies, wipes, cream etc. This doesn't just happen. Proctor and Gamble, Johnson & Johnson or Unilever etc. will have a deliberate strategy to garner your loyalty.

Attributes and Growth

Customer/user class driven businesses will have specific describable class(es) of customers/users who have common or similar needs. They're always looking (through great insight) to introduce new products or services. These products might be completely different and diverse.

Strategy Driven by Market Type

The two areas of excellence for market type are the same as for customer or user class. Companies who have selected market type as their future driving force must excel at:

1. Market research and
2. Customer loyalty

Consequently, market research and customer loyalty programmes must be outstanding. Market types can often be associated with proximity, for example schools, construction sites etc. They can also be clusters of individuals, for example pensioners, teenage football fans or work-from-home micro business owners.

Strategy Driven by Size, Growth and Profit

1. Portfolio Management

Many companies believe, at first, that they are profit-driven businesses. "Everyone wants to make a profit," I often hear when I deliver the Strategic Thinking Programme.

But it's not as simple as that.

More often than not, companies in this category are holding companies, conglomerates, VCs or private equity businesses. These companies specialise in building their portfolio of companies. What is absolutely critical for them is to standardise the way they manage their portfolio of businesses. They'll have a series of portfolio management frames, KPIs, planning and reporting systems. Their ability to manage the portfolio as effectively as possible is critical. They'll need to be able to on-board, sustain, scale and dispose of businesses as effectively as possible.

2. Asset Management

The companies are driven by the numbers and the overall value of the business as a whole, especially the value generated by its assets. Whether these be physical, data or intellectual assets.

The numbers run the show and those numbers must be moving in the appropriate direction. That's what defines a company driven by size, growth and profit.

Attributes and Growth

They may not necessarily have links between the businesses within the portfolio, but they might. They'll almost certainly want to cultivate a finely tuned radar or process to identify new targets. Once they've found potential acquisitions they will have a finely tuned scorecard to evaluate potential new acquisitions or investment opportunities.

Let's take some Virgin brands e.g. Virgin Media, Virgin Trains, Virgin Atlantic, Virgin Mobile and Virgin Holidays. They will have their own specific driving forces. However, the Virgin Group is almost certainly driven by size, growth and profit.

Future Strategic Profile (FSP)

There's only one way to decide your future driving force with any degree of confidence or certainty. To do this effectively, you have to step into the future. I shared earlier in the book the importance and significance of an organisation's current profile. A critical part of Strategic Thinking is to imagine in a degree of detail what the future profile of your organisation could be in order to give you the best chance of success in the *Future Business Arena.* To give it some more gravitas I call it your organisation's *Future Strategic Profile* (FSP). In essence an FSP is you and the team manifesting what your organisation will look like 3 years from now. You're painting a picture so to speak.

As with all things Strategic Thinking related, you need to harness what your SLT thinks, feels and believes. The future of your organisation depends on their engagement and commitment to deliver the results you need. This is always best achieved by galvanising all the key people to imagine what this FSP should look like. Critically, to go wide and deep you need to explore more than one option. We recommend the SLT design a few options of what the potential FSP could look like if your organisation chose 2 or 3 alternative driving forces.

This is how I recommend you approach it:

The facilitator will run through the 10 possible driving force candidates. Then ask the group to consider how the business might flourish going forward with each one of the potential driving force candidates. Through a process of elimination, you arrive at the most promising two or three. Often there is a standout favourite and frequently this is the current driving force. However, I encourage the group to choose two others which could take the business in an exciting new, fresh direction.

Once three driving force options are identified, break the whole group up into three breakout teams. Allocate a driving force to each team. At this point I make sure the CEO, MD or Managing Partner isn't allocated to a team; they're free to roam from group to group. The reason for this will become clear later. As mentioned previously, sometimes the SLT group size only lends itself to choosing two possible driving force candidates, and this is also absolutely fine.

Each team is then given the challenge over the next few hours of creating the *Potential Future Strategic Profile* or Concept (PFSP) for their business. Critically, they're looking into the future through the lens of a specific driving force. Depending on the industry sector, I usually recommend looking at a three year timeline. This could be longer if the dynamics of the industry are extremely capital intensive e.g. airline, hotel industry etc. It can help to write the PFSP from the perspective of being three years into the future, i.e. you've hopped onto a time machine and arrived three years into the future. I encourage the teams to write the PFSP by describing in outline terms what we look like 3 years in the future:

- What products or services are they selling? To which customers and users? In which industry sectors? And in which geographic areas?
- Over the three years what products, services, customers/user, industry sectors and geographical areas have they placed greater or less emphasis or focus on?
- Describe how they're leading the competitors by being world class in the two or three areas of excellence.
- What are the rules of the sandbox and how have they changed the game and leveraged their position in this new Business Arena?
- Are they a controller or influencer within the sandbox?
- What are the key numbers that they've achieved, for example turnover, gross margin, EBIT, market share etc.

As always with the Strategic Thinking Programme I invite each breakout team to present their vision of the future, their PFSP to the rest of the group in turn. Once every group has presented, then they vote. They all choose one PFSP and its underpinning driving force which they feel will bring the greatest success to the business. Which will create the strongest game-changer business? It's rarely unanimous, but usually circa 90% are clearly in favour of one of the PFSPs. It's important to work with the exceptions to understand their reasoning behind favouring another. Often it's because they really like an aspect of one of the other options. Often a compromise is found where we "drag and drop" that idea or feature into the winning PFSP. Everyone must and indeed always do arrive at a unanimous decision. Only with total and complete agreement and alignment can you successfully move forward to the next stage.

Myself or the facilitator will then produce a single page descriptor, capturing the essence of the winning PFSP, to produce the final draft Future Strategic Profile. In essence, I've distilled all the ambition and ideas that featured in the winning PFSP into a single compelling narrative. A FSP picture on a single page. It's no longer a potential candidate: the decision has been universally made. You are now a complete collective, 100% in agreement that this one page compelling picture is what we now need to build. The entire group will carefully scrutinise every word, make any final tweaks and then ALL sign it off – literally. You have your *Future Strategic Profile.*

You're now ready to enter part 3 and identify exactly what needs to happen and how you're going to deliver the FSP and future growth of the organisation. In other words, how are you now going to make this *Future Strategic Profile* a reality?

Key Takeaways

There are 10 potential driving forces for a business to choose from. Ideally, you'll follow the Strategic Thinking Programme to properly assess which future driving force will give your business the best chance of success in the Future Business Arena. As a group you're all 100% aligned behind a single Future Strategic Profile which you've all signed off.

Once that driving force has been settled on, the group *must* perfect a plan to become truly class leading in the two or three areas of excellence that underpin your chosen driving force. Only by doing this can you truly outthink, outpace and outmanoeuvre the competition.

Action Steps

1. Which of the 10 possible candidates is your organisation's current driving force?
2. How do you currently perform vs your competitors in the areas of excellence relating to your current driving force?
3. Keep in mind that it is always wise to choose your future driving force only once you've completed the first parts of the Strategic Thinking Programme. Which two alternative driving forces do you think could take your business to a whole new level?

MASTER YOUR
DRIVING FORCE'S
AREAS OF
EXCELLENCE
IN ORDER TO
MAKE YOUR
COMPETITIVE
POWER ALMOST
UNSTOPPABLE.

Part 4

The Three Lenses

In the Strategic Thinking Programme journey you should now have complete clarity and consensus on your:

Scan the QR code for this chapter's video

- Current Profile – success and failures.
- Sandbox – your extended marketplace and stakeholder map.
- Future Business Arena – clarity on your trading environment three years from now.
- Competitive landscape – your relative position vs direct and indirect competitors.
- Strengths, Weaknesses, Opportunities, Threats and Vulnerabilities.
- Future Driving Force has been selected.
- Future Strategic Profile has been signed-off.

So, you know where you are now and you know where you want to get to. You now need to get into the absolute detail of the ***What.*** What do you need to protect? What new stuff must you build?

What must you…

- *Defend* at all costs while you drive significant change through the business?
- Do that is new and different going forward, your new offensive strategy?
- Do to be truly world class at the important areas of excellence?
- Change to ensure you have the optimum Future Business Model steering your business?

Essentially, you will be brainstorming through three different lenses to flesh out all the stuff that needs to happen in order for you to successfully transition from where you are now to where you want to be.

If you haven't already gathered, I am an absolute advocate of structured brainstorming (or pelotoning). If you provide the participants with a frame with prompts rather than just a blank piece of paper you will see much greater quality and quantity of ideas generated. That's exactly what you do here with the three lenses approach. I separate the group into three teams to explore what needs to be in place in order to achieve the Future Strategic Profile

The three lenses are:

- Lens 1: Future Business Model
- Lens 2: Areas of Excellence
- Lens 3: Defensive and Offensive Strategic Objectives

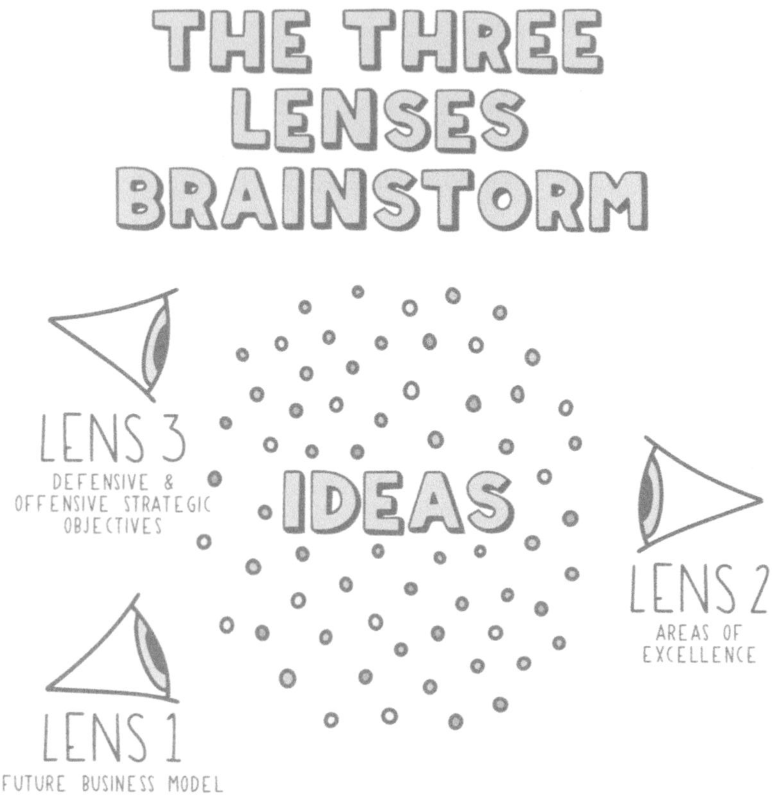

Lens #1: Future Business Model

All businesses have 10 component parts to their business model. The team has to consider how their own company's business model needs to evolve in order to deliver our FSP (Future Strategic Profile) effectively. The first team will work on what the future business model needs to look like.

These ten areas will look familiar to you. All of them match up with the ten potential driving forces, except for the last one which, in this case, is geographical location instead of size, growth and profit.

In the future business model, you need to look at *each* of these areas to ascertain what changes are required in order to move the business from its current business model to its future business model. Also take care to capture those current fundamentals to your business model that also need to be in place in the future business model.

It's also important to consider the implications on your people and team in each of the 10 areas that follow. Consider where you need to strengthen. What training needs to happen? How could engagement be achieved? What will it cost in terms of investment and resources (people are usually one of your main and most precious resources)? I've listed a few questions you may want to consider, but I'm sure you can identify many more.

#1 Technology and Know-How

What **tech and know-how** do you need to deploy going forward? Do you need to hire "enablers" that can facilitate the implementation of specific tech and know-how to bring your products to market? Do you need to fundamentally change from a legacy system that's been holding you back? Think about where the tech sits i.e. in the engine room, kitchen or front of house? Or both? How can technology or software be deployed to improve your proposition? Your processes? How do you engage with stakeholders?

Do you need to take out patents on anything? How can you protect your Intellectual Property or Know-How? How can you find out what you don't know and plug these gaps? You get the picture. If innovation is the life source of any successful organisation then this first area of the future business model is critical.

#2 Resources & Partners

What **resources** do you need to deploy to transition the business? Which **human resources** do you need? How can we attract and retain skilled workers in an evolving technological landscape? Do you need to hire a particular skill set or adopt a new company culture or attitude moving forward? What can be done to achieve this culture? How can you ensure you maintain optimum engagement and trust levels across the entire organisation?

Improving **resources** might mean training some of your people, or it might mean collaborating with new partners. It might mean looking at where you source some of your ingredients or your materials for your production, or the way you deliver your service. Are certain key resources going to be in short supply? Increase significantly in price? Are some key resources or materials considered poor for the planet? With the United Nations Sustainable Development Goals, you need to future-proof your organisation with the UN's 17 goals very much in front of mind.

Also, it's important to consider whether strategic partnerships might be better alternatives to building or maintaining your own solution. Think about whether riding somebody else's wave makes more sense.

#3 Production Capacity

Do you have sufficient, future-proof **production or operational capacity** to continue delivering your service or producing your goods? Where is the production capacity located? Do you need to centralise or decentralise? Do you need to become more agile and, if yes, *how* do you do that so you can launch new products more effectively? Can our machinery and systems be easily upgraded or repurposed to handle new products or increased volumes? How might market trends and customer needs evolve, and are you positioned to respond? Which emerging technologies (automation, IoT, AI, etc.) can you integrate to boost efficiency and capacity? How robust is your supply chain, and what risks might disrupt your production?

#4 Production Capability

See if you can find something, or a list of things, that will give you an edge over the competition. It could be a *unique* edge or a *relative* edge. Any trained, developed or acquired know-how that will give you a capability advantage over some or all your competitors. You may consider coming back to this after you've brainstormed potential new products and services. Then back fill the additional capabilities needed.

#5 Products and Services

Your products and services are the outcome of the previous four – technology & know-how, resources & partners, capacity and capability. Look at the **products and services** you need to develop in order to achieve your FSP. How are you going to create a continuous pipeline of innovation? How can you augment and improve the current offering?

How are you going to get a minimum viable product to market as quickly and effectively as possible? How are you going to score these, evaluate them and filter them so that you initially focus on the significant ones that will make a difference?

#6 Sales and Marketing

Number six and number seven should really be looked at *after* you've looked at eight, nine and ten.

How are you going to evolve the way you do your sales and marketing after establishing your ideal new customers and users, industry sectors and geographical areas?

What are you going to do differently? Consider all aspects of the marketing mix:

- Product (covered in #5)
- Place (covered next in #7)
- Price
- Promotion
- People

Under promotion look at future channels, social strategies, above the line, below the line, sponsorship, messaging, tone of voice etc.

Price is massively important and should include consideration into payment terms, price positioning vs competition etc.

For people, you should be considering all stakeholders, but especially your own people. This may overlap with #1 – resources.

#7 Distribution

Again, it's essential to come back to this one after looking at eight, nine and ten.

How are you going to distribute your products and services to the market once you've established who your new customers and users are going to be? Which industry sectors will you be busy in? What new geographical areas will you be reaching out to? How will you successfully penetrate these new territories? Is licensing an option?

Will you partner or collaborate with somebody else? Do you need to change something in your logistics supply chain? What about reverse logistics?

Try and imagine how you could do things differently to be more effective over the next two years or so. What could change the game and create real advantage and differentiation for you?

#8 Customers and Users

Who will be your customers and users in the future? How will you measure loyalty and delight? How will they want to be engaged? Where do they hang out physically and virtually? This will feed into other areas of the future business model.

#9 Industry Sectors and Markets

Which industry sectors and markets will you be targeting in the future? Which will be fast-growing? Which are most attractive for the proposition you're evolving? Considering your capacity and capability, are certain segments or sectors more suitable?

#10 Geographical Areas

Which geographical areas will you be targeting?

Go back and look at six and seven now to make sure you have those fully covered after looking at eight, nine and ten.

The lens #1 group effectively brainstorms the company's strategy by looking at the ten components through the lens of the future business model.

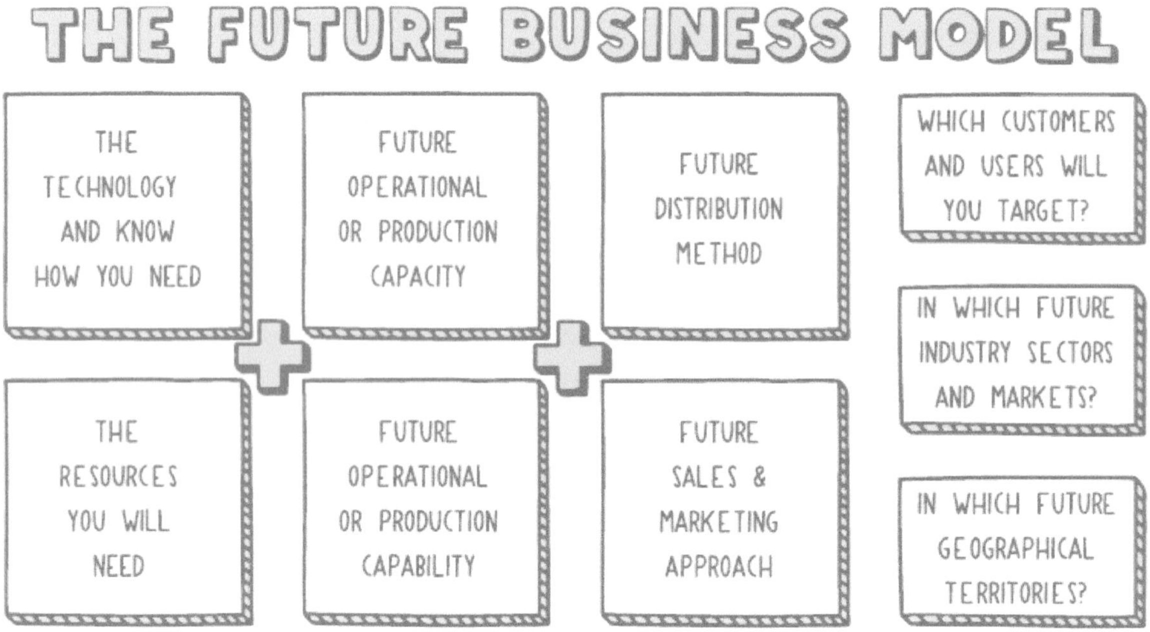

Fig 4.2c

Lens #2: Areas of Excellence

At this stage we know exactly what the two or three areas of excellence are.

Regardless of anything else you do, your company **must** be better in these two or three areas of excellence than your competition.

The primary objective of this team is to look at where the gaps are. Ideally, when deciding which group members are assigned to each team, it's really important to get people with first-hand knowledge of the areas of excellence so that they can speak with knowledge and authority. They might also be key personnel in leading the change after the workshop. The team needs to take a *realistic* look at where it is now, and then needs to look at what it needs to do in order to be *exceptional* in the future.

As you have probably come to expect, there's a formula and a precise set of steps to achieve excellence.

1. Capability

The first thing is to look at your current capability. Where are you truly today?

It's imperative to be completely honest about the answers obtained here. Nothing will be gained by overstating the current situation. Indeed, it might end up harming you here because you won't take proper stock of where you are and so won't know what you need to do to get better and to be where you need to be.

The team should discuss the point openly and freely, with no judgment, so that you know your starting point, your limitations, what is currently restricting you and where your competitors are performing better. It's likely that the person(s) responsible for the status quo are in this team. They must feel confident to speak freely about what's not as good as it could or should be. They must avoid being defensive and start justifying or defending the current reality. This is the moment to reset and reshape.

2. What does awesome look like?

Now the team asks itself, "What does awesome *look* like? What does world class look like for that particular area of excellence?"

Asking yourself these two questions creates a gap: you know where you are, and you now know where you're trying to be. Try to get into as much granular detail as possible. The group is effectively brainstorming all the new exciting developments and changes that need to happen in order to be excellent and significantly better than the competition.

3. How are you going to get there?

We need to identify and prioritise the gaps between our current capabilities and the desired capabilities. Consider what training and development is needed. Perhaps new recruitment is required. Do you just need some temporary consultancy expertise? Do you need to invest in systems, people and infrastructure? Do you need to pool efforts and establish a centre of excellence?

4. What are the precise deliverables?

Finally, the team needs to ask itself what the *precise* deliverables are. Who will be accountable and responsible for these deliverables? How long will it take to come up with and deliver necessary change?

What budget would be required to deliver this strategic change you need to close these gaps?

The above 4 steps must be carried out for each of the two or three areas of excellence.

Lens #3: Defensive and Offensive Strategic Objectives

The third team must focus on defensive and offensive strategic objectives.

This team must identify the critical areas of the current business that must be defended at all costs. These are the products or services that need to be continuously evolved and developed because they're key to both securing the future you want but also maintaining the momentum today.

You must continue to keep customers through delivering expected delight. Similarly, you must keep markets and geographical areas whose contributions we simply cannot do without. Critically, you must also consider your key people. Who are the key people in the organisation that you must keep? Whose committed engagement is critical to both today and tomorrow?

It's important to consider how you can continuously measure that you are successfully defending these key positions. For example, sales volume and revenue, satisfaction index and employee engagement scores etc. You have to ensure the organisation continues its incremental momentum by defending all the key elements identified.

In parallel, this team needs to consider what new progression needs to happen? What new hills must we conquer? This is the all-important other side of the coin – the change that you need to drive.

The new products and services to be developed? The new customers and users to be attracted and won over? The new industry sectors and markets and new geographical territories? What are the gaps in your know-how and capabilities? Effectively, what new ground do you need to capture in order to attain the Future Strategic Profile we've chosen?

Again, it's really important that you identify measurements so that you can track your progress.

Defence and offence is as important in a business context as it is on the sports field.

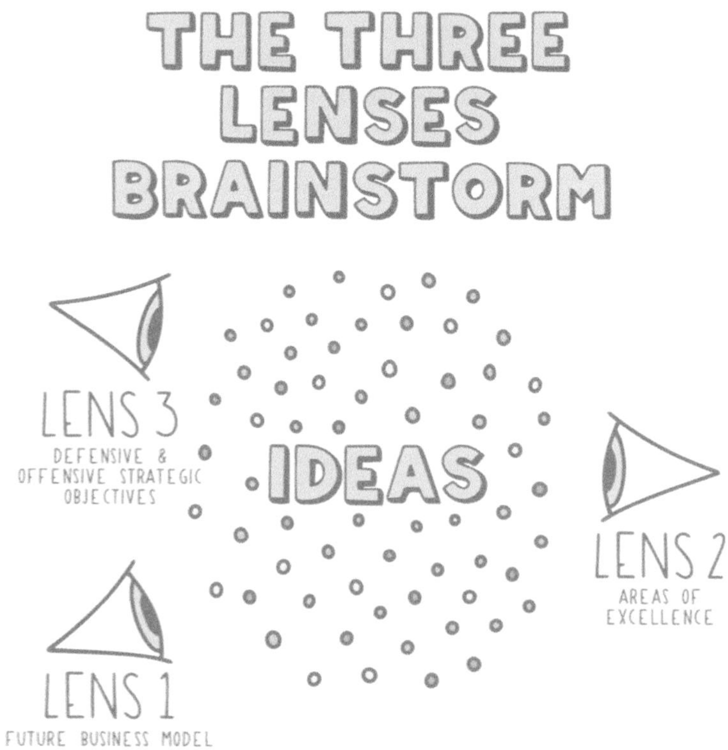

Fig 4.1c

Making sense of the three lens output

The three teams will yield an incredible amount of powerful ideas through the structured three lens brainstorming. Expect to see a significant amount of duplication, which is fine. This reinforces the importance of alignment in the teams' thinking. What's key is that when these ideas are assembled and sorted into clusters, that's where the magic starts to happen. This is the start as our strategy begins to take shape.

At this point the excitement in the room is palpable, but so is the sense of overwhelm. "How do we start to make sense of this?" "Where do we start?" "Who's going to deliver all this?"

This is when the workshop facilitator earns their fee. It's a real skill and they'll draw upon years of experience. As you'd expect, I've developed a process for doing this effectively.

What you want to do now is **cluster the ideas** into a few clearly defined ***critical issues***. Ideally, you want to end up with no more than six ***critical issues***. Fig 4.1c illustrates the cumulated ideas that are currently randomly assembled as a result of the three lens brainstorming. We now have to identify the broad headings of the critical issues (or significant projects).

Clearly the first two or three critical issues are going to be the areas of excellence. For the sake of illustrating the process, let's imagine you've chosen service as your driving force. Your first critical issue is going to be service development. You have a significant head start to this critical issue because one of the teams already brainstormed numerous ideas to make our service development world class. You then go through all the other outputs from the other two teams and write a "1" next to any ideas that will also contribute to the service development critical issue project. Then you identify critical issue ***#2 – sales and service.*** I've worked with many groups that chose to split these into two separate critical issues as the size of the challenge and importance warranted clear focus on each. As before, start with the output from the areas of excellence team and augment it with the sales and service related ideas from the other two breakout teams. It's now becoming clear (as demonstrated in fig 4.5c) that the wealth of ideas generated in the brainstorm are rapidly becoming clustered. At this stage all the ideas relating to the two or three areas of excellence are now clustered.

By now, the facilitator will have a sense of the next two or three critical issues. I've personally completed hundreds of the critical issues formulation sessions. I often find that there's a "people" critical issue: an organisation's culture, trust and engagement. Operational efficiency and effectiveness also often appears as a critical issue topic. Governance is also a recurring critical issue I've frequently seen. The facilitator will discuss their thinking with the entire group and then the clustering continues until all or nearly all the ideas have been allocated to a critical issue.

I often encounter a few outliers which don't sit in any of the identified critical issues. These are placed in the appropriate area of the future business model and the functional head responsible for this will take on the responsibility of exploring the idea. So, nothing is lost, nothing slips through the cracks, every single idea is captured and will be explored and if it has merit will form part of the game-changing strategy which is now starting to take shape.

Fig 4.5c

So, you now have your critical issues, you know how many you have, you've named them and allocated all the ideas to each critical issue. The next step is when the strategy really does start to take shape and come alive.

Nailing Your Critical Issues

Now, the group splits into teams to flesh out each critical issue using the frame fig 4.6. You'll work with the CEO/Managing Partner to ensure you get the right people in the right critical issue teams. From the work carried out previously in the three lens exercise each critical issue team will work with the ideas allocated to their own critical issue.

Scan the QR code for this heading's video

Each team will begin by articulating what success will look like or what the optimum desired outcome is for that specific critical issue. As with the FSP, I recommend writing in the future tense. For example if the critical issue is all about more effective sales and marketing.

By the end of 2026 the company will have:

- Revenues in excess of $500m @ gross margin of 45%.
- Min. 10% market share in our European markets
- Min 3% market share in the new emerging North American market
- Less than 2% customer attrition.

The more precise the better, you don't want ambiguity or wriggle room. Also, you want the outcomes to be measurable and ideally include a financial impact on the business. This could be revenue, EBIT or even cost reduction.

Once the teams have agreed the optimum outcome of their critical issue, they then craft the deliverables that need to happen in order for the outcome(s) to be achieved. Then they consider who should own each deliverable and what a reasonable timeframe could look like. Finally, they document all the contributors to the critical issue and decide who should have the responsibility to drive and deliver all these important deliverables that make up this important project (critical issue).

Once all the teams have completed the critical issue frame, each team will present their critical issue to the rest of the group. As always with the Strategic Thinking Process, this playback is important to get buy-in and to identify any duplication or dependencies between the deliverables of the various critical issues..

Before the workshop is complete it's important to assign an overall leader for each critical issue. It's always preferable that the leaders are chosen from the team that worked on that particular critical issue and have been present throughout the Strategic Thinking workshop.

These critical issues collectively represent the roadmap to reach your Future Strategic Profile. The Future Strategic Profile represents how you are going to change the game and significantly grow your business.

We now have the start of the Strategic Plan.

Key Takeaways

Future business model, areas of excellence, and offensive and defensive objectives dovetail to produce an actionable strategy that can take your business to where it needs to be. Expect lots of duplication, that's good, it shows alignment of thinking.

Each lens requires in-depth work, preferably done in a team. By brainstorming through each specific lens separately you can identify a wealth of valuable ideas.

Once all three lenses have been worked out completely, try to cluster the output into a maximum of six critical issues. *That* is your strategy starting to take clear shape.

Any residual ideas form part of your future business model, under the control of the functional head for that area.

Action Steps

1. Have a go at brainstorming through the 3 lenses'.
2. Consider what the critical issues to be addressed at your organisation could be.

THE BEST
TEACHERS ARE
THOSE WHO
SHOW YOU
WHERE TO
LOOK, BUT DON'T
TELL YOU WHAT
TO SEE.

The Power of the Strategic Filter

Imagine the impact if every director, manager or budget holder had a single page, on their desk, wall or in their top drawer, called the "Strategic Filter". A single page which would help guide their decision-making. If they all had the same strategic filter it would rapidly align all budgetary and resource decisions to support the businesses strategy.

I've seen the strategic filter have an incredibly empowering impact across entire organisations. Managers have challenged previously "sacred cows" and said, "No we're no longer going to do this". "If it doesn't pass through the filter, we're not going to do it".

Essentially, the strategic filter is a series of questions relating to the new strategy of the business. It can only be produced after the workshop has concluded. So before committing to spend money, allocate resources or apply some focused effort, all managers, directors and budget holders should run it through the strategic filter.. If it doesn't score any "yeses" then we probably shouldn't do it.

The net result of such a company-wide filter would be **faster, more accurate and appropriate decision-making, less wastage, saving time, money and effort and significantly faster overall progress**.

There are three distinct advantages to having a strategic filter as described above in your business:

1. No more wasting time and money

Initiatives and trivial tasks which have no impact on your business strategy should be stopped in their tracks by the strategic filter.

2. Saying "No" becomes so much easier

If an idea, expense or event doesn't pass through your strategic filter, then the answer is "No". You simply don't do it, and nobody can argue with it.

You are effectively empowering your people to say "NO".

3. The strategic filter helps you stay focused

One of the biggest challenges facing organisations when they have a clear strategy is actually delivering it. How does the saying go, "Success is 10% strategy and 90% execution". The day to day reality of operating a business often gets in the way and distracts or worse derails the strategy. Keeping a laser-like focus on delivering our strategy and getting to the Future Strategic Profile as quickly as possible is key.

A strategic filter keeps the team focused and dramatically improves your chances of executing the company's strategy and arriving at your Future Strategic Profile sooner.

How to design a strategic filter

I wish I could show you a shortcut, but I can't. Because there isn't one.

The strategic filter is one of the outcomes of going through the entirety of the Strategic Thinking Programme as laid out in this book.

You have everything you need in this book to carry out such a programme.

Let's assume that you and your extended SLT have completed the Strategic Thinking Programme;

- Success & Failures
- Sandbox
- Competition Audit
- Future Business Arena
- SWOT+
- Driving Force
- Future Strategic Profile
- Future Business Model
- Areas of Excellence
- Defensive and Offensive Objectives
- Identified and scoped the Critical issues

The strategic filter is where you take the key elements of your strategy and specifically those critical issues and detail them appropriately under the following three headings;

- Does the opportunity……
- Does this opportunity leverage our areas of excellence….
- Does this opportunity enhance our need to…..

Effectively you've got to capture the headlines of your strategy and the deliverables within the critical issues and list them in the appropriate section above. Then to the right hand side there is a simple Yes/No tick box.

All significant investments of time, money and effort should be passed through the filter. If it receives one or more yeses then it's contributing to the strategy so we should probably do it. If it doesn't receive a single yes, then you probably shouldn't be doing it.

Key Takeaways

Every action your company takes from now on should align with its new strategic plan.

The simplest way to achieve this alignment is to develop a strategic filter and distribute it throughout the organisation.

Strategic filters help SLTs and managers keep a laser focus and will save time, resources and money. It makes saying "no" so much easier, and helps the entire company stay focused.

Action Steps

1. Can you think of an event or an expense that you're no longer convinced is appropriate for you to continue with?
2. At your next team meeting ask the team to think of instances where there was a stalemate, where the decision to go/not go was put on the back burner.

Part 5

Bonus Tracks

This section of the book is where I've placed the "bonus tracks". These are the slightly random things which I think are thought-provoking or simply a bit of fun.

Enjoy….

The CEO Self-Assessment

It's not easy being the leader of a business. It can be lonely and isolating. Assembling a stellar team is important. Harnessing that team to both develop and deliver the strategy in order to scale the business is critical.

For several years now, the World Economic Forum in Davos has identified that Critical Thinking is the number one skill leaders must perfect.

A lack of strategy makes the team uneasy because it is virtually the same as not having a destination at all. It's like saying "I think I know where I'm going, but I'm lost".

I've had the pleasure and good fortune, as co-founder of peer2peer global and Managing Partner of DPI Europe, to work with so many incredible leaders in businesses in a plethora of different industries.

It is that very experience which led me to put together the CEO Self-Assessment.

If, as a leader, you often find yourself believing that you're not optimising your strategy for *growth* as effectively as you could be, there are ten questions you can ask yourself to tell if you have it spot-on, or if there's room for improvement.

These questions comprise the CEO Self-Assessment.

In order to get the most from the CEO Self-Assessment, answer this from the perspective of the **current reality** in your business, NOT from the perspective of what you think the answer should be.

My intention in writing this book was twofold:

1. To empower CEOs, founders, entrepreneurs and senior leaders to recognise the importance of Strategic Thinking and to share the know-how on how to run a Strategic Thinking process from start to finish
2. To codify and delineate the Strategic Thinking Programme accurately and efficiently in this book so that the knowledge of it gets spread far and wide, thereby assisting businesses to succeed.

Obviously, if you're not a CEO you can still have a crack at the survey. If you feel your company would benefit then ask the SLT and the boss to have a go themselves.

The CEO Self-Assessment

#1

Do you regularly (at least every three years) have a broad and deep strategic time-out with your extended leadership team to nail your strategy?

#2

Is your board primarily focused on numbers and financials rather than on Critical Thinking and good Strategic Thinking?

#3

Do you suffer from planning numbrosis?

I.e. A strategic process that's run or underpinned by finance on an excel spreadsheet

#4

Are you delighted by the level of stretch and ambition in your strategic plan?

(why would you settle for anything less than "delighted"?)

#5

Is your strategy clearly articulated and understood by your senior leadership team, your management and by your staff?

#6

Is your senior leadership team *completely aligned* and in *total agreement* regarding the priorities and focus of your business?

#7

Does your senior team *react* to challenges and changes rather than *anticipating* and positively *driving* change?

#8

Do you believe there is an engagement gap between your senior leadership team and their direct reports?

#9

Does the (1) strategy, (2) action plan, (3) execution and (4) delivery happen as effectively as you want it to?

#10

Do you ever feel isolated as a leader of your business?

Companies work best when they are operating as a *team*, when everybody is on the same page and the SLT has bought into the strategy and is driving it home to completion because they had a crucial part in developing it – and because they *believe* in it.

DIY or DIP?

I wrote this book because I've been regularly disappointed with business books that show a little ankle but don't actually drop their trousers (metaphorically). They're extremely conceptual. You get into the theory, they unlock your thinking, but, critically, stop short of actually helping you get it done yourself. This book is deliberately transparent and if you follow it with your extended SLT you will learn the fundamentals that will help you to develop an excellent strategy to grow your business.

However, many CEOs recognise that it's too important to **DIY** (do it yourself). They recognise that they must **DIP** (Do It Properly): bring me or one of our team into their business and deliver the entire programme harnessing their extended SLT. We've helped over 3500 businesses worldwide, time and time again, to design and build growth strategies to outthink, outpace and outmanoeuvre their competition.

So, I'm just putting it here that I would, of course, be delighted to assist you if you wish. Simply go to www.piesorpiecharts.com and reach out to me and the team.

EVERY GREAT ARTIST HAS A CLOSET FULL OF BAD PAINTINGS.

The Growth Grid

An organisation's growth is a flight. Sometimes the flight is effortless and organic.

At other times, organisations need to draw on specific skill sets and expertise to consciously drive change in order to remain competitive and deliver growth.

The biggest trap organisations fall into is failure to execute the correct change effectively. We've all seen those business school mantras "10% strategy, 90% execution" etc. Well it's very true. Many, many times in my career I've experienced a great strategy fail because it couldn't get out of the starting blocks. If only there was a simple framework to follow to guide businesses to take their well thought-through strategy and execute it speedily and effectively.

This is why I developed the Growth Grid in 2015 as a lite very simple frame – to provide executives and managers with a simple workable 7 stage frame to follow. If the leadership team follows the 7 stages of the Growth Grid, the end to end delivery of strategy will improve dramatically.

The Growth Grid isn't rocket science, but its simplicity makes it deployable and highly effective. In the example below I refer to the SLT as the SMT (Senior Management Team) in this context they're interchangeable.

Only 7 Steps to Guaranteed Growth

Achieving growth is not complicated. All that is required is doing seven things, and doing them well.

I can 100% guarantee you this: If you execute every single step of this Growth Grid's seven elements, you will achieve growth. You and the leadership team need to:

- Make sure you involve the extended senior leadership team in the formulation of your sustainable growth strategy. If they're involved it's going to be a better, well thought-through strategy and they're more likely to completely buy into it.
- You need to make sure you deploy a robust and effective framework to guide the team on the Strategic Thinking journey (see parts 2, 3 and 4 in this book).
- Make sure the chosen strategy is translated into detailed critical issues which form the skeleton of your action plan.
- You need to make sure that the necessary resources are made available to the project teams responsible for delivering the action plan.
- Make sure the project teams have all the necessary skills to deliver the project.

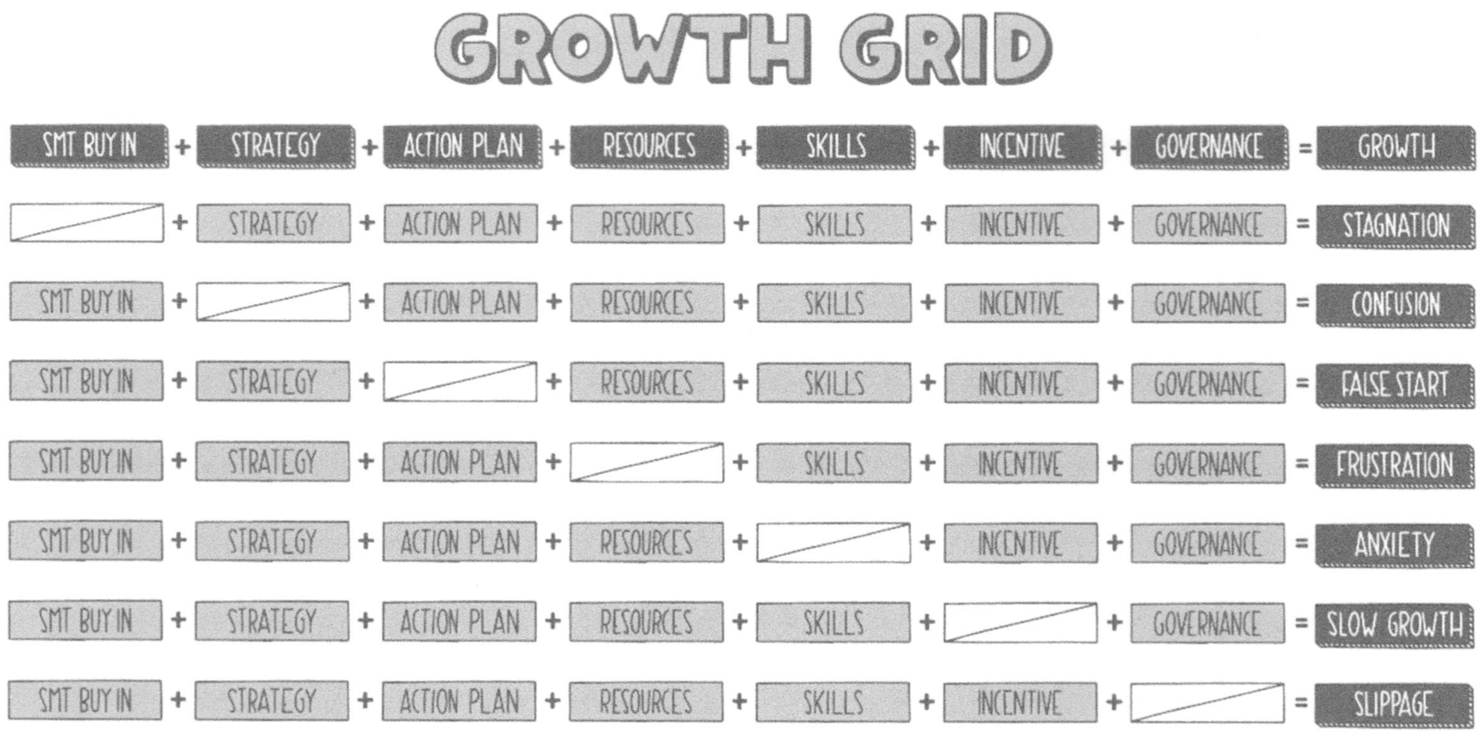
GROWTH GRID
SMT BUY IN + STRATEGY + ACTION PLAN + RESOURCES + SKILLS + INCENTIVE + GOVERNANCE = GROWTH
+ STRATEGY + ACTION PLAN + RESOURCES + SKILLS + INCENTIVE + GOVERNANCE = STAGNATION
SMT BUY IN + + ACTION PLAN + RESOURCES + SKILLS + INCENTIVE + GOVERNANCE = CONFUSION
SMT BUY IN + STRATEGY + + RESOURCES + SKILLS + INCENTIVE + GOVERNANCE = FALSE START
SMT BUY IN + STRATEGY + ACTION PLAN + + SKILLS + INCENTIVE + GOVERNANCE = FRUSTRATION
SMT BUY IN + STRATEGY + ACTION PLAN + RESOURCES + + INCENTIVE + GOVERNANCE = ANXIETY
SMT BUY IN + STRATEGY + ACTION PLAN + RESOURCES + SKILLS + + GOVERNANCE = SLOW GROWTH
SMT BUY IN + STRATEGY + ACTION PLAN + RESOURCES + SKILLS + INCENTIVE + = SLIPPAGE

Figure 1.2

- It's vital that all involved in delivering the projects are properly incentivised to do so.
- Finally, throughout the execution journey, proper governance of each project and the total programme needs to be effective.

If all of the above seven elements are in place, then GROWTH is certain. If one or more elements isn't adequately covered then the necessary innovation and change is unlikely to happen and your desired growth will be threatened.

Let's take a look at each element in more detail.

SLT (Senior Leadership Team) Buy-In – Stagnation

Failures or weaknesses in SLT buy-in for your strategy or plan will result in the stagnation of the strategy, plan or overall company performance.

If your SLT doesn't buy into the strategy – if they don't *own* it – you will have stagnation.

The hard truth of the matter is that, if you don't get a complete SLT buy-in of your project, individual members of the SLT will push back against forward progress. They'll block it. They might even privately like to see it fail just to prove a point. I've seen this happen first hand when a client brought in a lean process improvement consultancy. A number of key directors were not happy about this decision. The incumbent leadership team seemed to almost pray every day that the project would fail and that they'd be given the reins again to try to fix the situation themselves.

This is indeed the biggest problem with bringing in external content consultants such as the Big Name Consultancy Companies.

One of the most significant risks of doing that is that either all or some of the SLT will feel resentful about it. A vote of no confidence if you like. You may even lose some of your best people, who take their talents elsewhere.

The consequence is stagnation.

There *is* a time and place for content consulting companies. That time and place is when there is indeed a gap in knowledge or capability within your own leadership team, and that content consulting company then fills that gap. But, critically, make sure that all key members of the extended leadership team are involved in the decision and selection process of the content specialists. Make sure they're also *dovetailed* into the project and involved throughout. They'll then feel part of the decision making and subsequent success.

These are things which the team itself should be doing! Putting strategy and innovation into the hands of an external company only makes your business *reliant* on that company, and doesn't allow it to learn to stand on its own two feet and compete with the best of them. Always try to ensure your team learns from the specialists so that next time, potentially, they can change the tyre themselves.

Get your leadership team to buy into the strategy or project.

LIFT THE FOG
OF UNCERTAINTY
THEN PLOT THE
PERFECT
COURSE FOR
YOUR BUSINESS.

Strategy – Confusion

Failures or weaknesses in an organisation's strategy will result in confusion or much worse.

Either the strategy hasn't been made clear, or it's the wrong strategy altogether.

I make no apologies for repeating myself – following a rigorous Strategic Thinking process, which asks great questions in the correct sequence *WILL* result in better levels of individual and collective thinking. The consequence of this better thinking is a clearer vision of what you all want to build and a clear strategy on how to get there.

If you don't deploy a good Strategic Thinking process, then, as a minimum, the result is confusion amongst leadership and other stakeholders. People down the line won't understand it, won't understand the vision or the strategy. They'll all have their own interpretation, they'll have mixed messages. The leadership team will be divided and possibly divisive.

Ensure that your overall strategy has been worked out effectively and clearly by the SLT and then get this strategy communicated *clearly* down the line. Create clear communications, if necessary, to ensure that everyone in the company knows where it's headed and so don't end up bumping into each other in the process of trying to execute a confused strategy.

If the strategy is confused, the business, at best, is going to limp along, but will most likely fail.

A famous example is in the logistics space around 2007 to 2011. I make this assessment as a professional outsider looking in. For many years TNT Express had held an enviable position as the quality player and the most profitable in the delivery sector. Reporting consistent growth and 6% ROS (return on sales) year after year.

During this period, when every other post and express parcel business was preparing for and moving into B2C (Business to Consumer) deliveries , Marie-Christine Lombard, the CEO of TNT, proclaimed that they were going to stay B2B (Business to Business) and be the best at B2B. This strategy had served them well for many years. The one massive oversight was that the market was moving rapidly to B2C. The rest is history and TNT was eventually acquired by FedEx. TNT had ignored the dramatic shift in their Future Business Arena. There are so many examples of big businesses which decided their best strategy was to stay as they are as it had always worked for them: Kodak, Vodafone, Woolworths, Blockbuster to name just a few seemingly unassailable behemoths. They had been so successful they thought they couldn't lose – and where are they all now?

Examples of a confused or poor strategy as a result of NOT deploying an effective Strategic Thinking process include:

- Kodak failing to leverage their own digital imaging breakthrough. They suppressed it because they didn't want to erode their film processing revenues, buried their heads in the sand and watched the rest of the world embrace digital.

- Blockbuster – everybody else seemed to see that the massive adoption of home broadband and improved mobile signal 3G led to the advent of streaming platforms for music and film. They had the means to buy the emerging disruptor Netflix, but didn't.
- Disposable plastic bags – remember them? It was unbelievably predictable that legislation could/will be passed outlawing the millions of disposable bags being issued for free by supermarkets all over the world. First the bag tax, then the ban.
- Single use plastic bottles will follow very shortly. Ireland has already served notice of an imminent ban. Recycled bottles are now prominent in all the big water brands.

In stark contrast, DPD Group's decision to embrace B2C from 2008 as a direct result of a 3-day DPI Strategic Thinking Workshop was the start of an incredible 12-year journey which has seen them rise from relative obscurity to Europe's number one parcel company. The fastest growing, most profitable, with the best technology and the best service.

If the strategy is not good or not clear, the result is confusion and often eventual failure.

Action Plan – False Starts

If the action plan is missing, you will get false starts, no starts, or simply no action at all.

"We've got a great strategy!" the team proclaims, but they haven't decided:

- **Who** is going to do it?
- **How** is it going to happen?
- **Who** is going to resource it?
- **Who** is going to lead it?
- **Who** is going to pay for it?
- **What will the deliverables** be?
  KPIs – How do you measure success?

To achieve growth, your strategy requires a *clear* action plan.

Some of the critical things a *clear* action plan encompasses are:

- Who owns the opportunity or challenge? In other words, who will be the executive sponsor? Every critical issue should be adapted into a critical project (see part 4 – Critical Issues). Executive sponsorship and a clear project leader are very important to ensure leadership and accountability.
- Who's on the team? It's vitally important to establish a small effective team that covers all the key functions/areas needed to deliver all elements of the strategy. Tip-select your team after you've framed the whole project.

- What does success look like? "Start with the end in mind" – Steven Covey, spot on in my view. Describe this success as clearly and unambiguously as possible.
- What are the deliverables?
- Break down all the steps necessary for each deliverable.
- Who needs to lead each deliverable? These people make up the team.

What often happens is that the leadership team has a fantastic strategic retreat, hosted by Big Name Consultancy Co.

Big Name Consultancy Co then leaves riding their horse over the hill into the setting sun. Six months later, the output documents and PowerPoint slides are collecting dust. Nothing has happened. The SLT sits around scratching their heads wondering why nothing happened.

To achieve steady progress and growth, a *clear* action plan must be in place.

Resources – Frustration

Failures in resources result in frustration.

So, you gather your SLT and other key people. You follow an effective proven framework. You translate the chosen vision and strategy into a clear action plan consisting of critical issues and projects. So what's next?

Next, you fail to give them the resources they need to execute that action plan. This is one of the seven deadly sins of growing a business. Starve the execution team from the critical resources needed to complete the job.

The result is frustration – massive frustration.

Resources can be:

- Money
- Time
- People
- Solutions
- Software
- Tech
- Etc.

If the project is not resourced correctly, enormous frustration can ensue.

I recall being invited into a fast-growing e-commerce business in early 2017. A Private Equity (PE) house had taken a significant stake in the business and was becoming increasingly inpatient and concerned that the well thought-through strategy hadn't gathered the traction they had expected. The strategy and action plan were sound. When we held a programme review meeting it was clear where the issue was. Due to pressure on short-term EBIT return, to satisfy the PE shareholder the executive team had elected to cancel some critical insight which would have enabled a better, sharper digital marketing strategy. As a result, time and money were wasted needlessly. The execution team knew it was a mistake, which is why the resource issue was identified so promptly.

Make sure that you provide people with the required resources to execute the action plan.

Skills – Anxiety

Inappropriate, inadequate or missing skills can result in anxiety.

This follows on directly from resources because one of the resources is people.

I often see organisations compromising on the make-up of critical teams assigned to deliver critical projects. If they are lacking a specialist skill or know-how they all too often compromise and 'make do' with the nearest best fit internal candidate. Sometimes it only slightly impacts the outcome but occasionally the result can be massively off target. If the skills, know-how or experience don't exist within the team, go find it from outside. This is when "content consultants" can be an absolute must.

If you're asking people to do things they are not skilled or capable of doing, such as:

- Project management
- Sales excellence training
- Complex data analysis
- Customer experience modelling
- Touchpoint analysis etc.

Anxiety levels will go through the roof and your growth strategy will stall completely.

Your project teams need to have the skills, know-how, confidence and training to properly execute all elements diligently, competently and speedily.

Incentive – Slow Growth

Lack of incentive results in slow growth.

Hundreds of white papers, books, conferences, businesses, in fact a whole industry has blossomed by specialising in unlocking the mysteries of engagement and motivation. We all know that money and bonuses play some part, but, often, that's a very small part of what drives an individual to be extremely motivated. Individual and collective flow is critical. When somebody is in a state of flow they need little incentive to drive on and deliver change. If they're taken out of flow, then you must have incentives in place to motivate them and sustain levels of effort.

It is very important that all key members of the various project teams involved in delivering or executing the growth strategy of the organisation are totally engaged and motivated. In most organisations, members of the critical project teams have this responsibility in addition to the "day-to-day role". It's additional. I've seen many occasions where these individuals have been engaged in their day-to-day delivery, because that's where they're rewarded, recognised or most engaged and in flow. It's so important that all involved in critical projects receive a motivation and engagement "reboot". They have to be completely engaged and in flow when working on the project.

If someone's bonus is paid to deliver XYZ but is not paid to deliver this new strategic programme or strategic change, they will always default and deliver XYZ.

In the end, they'll say, "I'm sorry. I just didn't have the time."

What they're really saying is, "The time I had, I chose to spend it elsewhere because you didn't incentivise me to focus on this." They may also be telling you the truth, if their original job was full time engagement they need a resource, such as an assistant, to cover the stuff they can delegate in order to execute their part in the new Strategic Plan.

If you want to drive change, it's absolutely critical to motivate people to deliver that change.

The motivation isn't always necessarily financial. It depends on the circumstances and scenario at hand.

That motivation could be financial, a bigger bonus, a trip to Vegas if it's delivered on time, more time off – whatever.

If the proper incentives are in place, as well as all the previous steps of the Growth Grid, then growth is not only steady but also *rapid.*

Governance – Slippage

Without proper governance, you get slippage.

A strategy that is going to change an organisation is very rarely a single project. It's usually a load of projects, often with dependencies; often with managing existing systems until the new systems are ready.

Proper effective governance is absolutely key. If done rigorously it will flush out any shortfalls with action planning, resources, skills, know-how and incentives.

All of this must be governed.

Having proper governance and proper programme management across an organisation is vital.

If you don't have this, almost certainly everything will slip, and the change won't happen on time, if at all.

Strategy Is Not Complicated

Strategy is not complicated. However, the vast majority of consultancy firms do go out of their way to *make* it complicated.

Too many consultants want you to pay them to do strategy for you. They want to maintain themselves as the aggregator of knowledge and know-how. They'll often deploy a strategy with you that focuses on giving themselves more opportunities to earn, which may not be the best thing for you and your business.

I'm obsessed with demystifying and making the complex as simple as possible. That's why I developed the Growth Grid. It's actually very simple and very logical.

What we believe at peer2peer is that, if you get these seven elements right, you will be successful, and your organisation will achieve growth.

Key Takeaways

The Growth Grid is a simple practical tool.

Get all seven elements of the Growth Grid right and you will achieve growth.

If you see any of the negative consequences (anxiety, frustration, stagnation, etc.) in your project, look for which of the seven elements is/are missing and get them fixed immediately.

Don't shove strategy down your leadership team's throats. Empower them to come up with their own strategy collectively.

Make sure the strategy is correct, clear and understood all the way down the line.

Ensure your action plan is *clear* and encompasses all the necessary aspects to execute the strategy.

Make sure your team has the resources needed to execute the action plan. Resources are not only people but also know-how, tools, software, finances, time etc.

The people you choose for a task must have the skills and be competent in the execution of that task. Failing to use people trained or skilled in a specific area will lead to anxiety and slow-down.

No incentive or the wrong incentive can lead to slow growth. Incentives are not always financial.

Strategic changes usually involve far more than one project. Proper governance of all that is going on is necessary to avoid slippage.

And, last, but far from least: Strategy is not complicated!

Let's say that again: *Strategy is not complicated!*

Get Started

Here are some quick and easy things you can do *right now* to start implementing the Growth Grid in your business and so solidify the knowledge of this chapter in your mind.

1. Reach out to me and the team at www.piesorpiecharts.com to get a copy of the Growth Grid frame.
2. Distribute a copy of the Growth Grid to every member of the SLT and other key people who lead projects in your business.
3. Ask them to think of a recent project that transcended most/all of the organisation. Invite them to score out of 10 each of the seven elements and send the responses directly to you (10 being world class).
4. Aggregate all responses and then meet all involved to discuss.
5. Put steps in place to make sure all projects are fully compliant with the Growth Grid.

Did you ever meet Rudyard Kipling's smarter brother?

Rudyard Kipling had a very smart brother. He wrote his own version of "If", remarkably similar to Rudyard's poem by the same name. (That poem, incidentally, was voted Britain's favourite poem in a 1995 BBC opinion poll.[14])

He was ahead of his time…

[14] https://poets.org/poem/if

"IF" – YOU USE CRITICAL THINKING

IF YOU AND YOUR PEOPLE CAN HARNESS BRAIN POWER
WHEN YOUR COMPETITORS STRUGGLE TO THINK.
IF YOU AND YOUR TEAM CAN SHARE LEADERSHIPS STRAIN
WHILE OTHERS STAY IN SILOS AND SINK.

IF YOUR LEADERSHIP TEAM STARTS TO ALIGN
YOU'LL OUT-THINK RIVALS, SENDING THEM INTO DECLINE.
IF YOU WORK TOGETHER – THERE'S NO MORE FRICTION.
COHESION CREATES A UNITED VISION.

IF YOU CAN ENCOURAGE COLLABORATION IN YOUR TEAMS
YOU'LL INSPIRE IDEAS AND REALISE DREAMS.
IF YOU ACKNOWLEDGE EACH WRONG TURN AS YOU PROGRESS,
YOU CELEBRATE FAILURE AS PART OF SUCCESS.

IF YOU'RE DRIVING DISRUPTION WITH OUR PROCESS FOR STEALTH,
YOU'LL HAVE SUSTAINABLE INNOVATION FOR CORPORATE RUDE HEALTH.
IF YOUR FRAMEWORKS INDUCE COLLABORATION AND FLOW,
YOURE ENGAGING TALENT AND FOSTERING GROWTH.

IF YOU CAN IDENTIFY THE PLAYERS IN YOUR SANDBOX,
THIS KNOWLEDGE BRINGS POWER, THIS WISDOM – IT ROCKS.
DRIVING FORCE SELECTION AND FUTURE PROFILE DELIVER
AND YOUR COMPETITION WILL SOON TIRE AND WITHER.

IF YOU CAN DO ALL OF THIS
YOU'LL HAVE MASTERED CRITICAL THINKING
AND WHAT'S MORE
GROWTH AND SUCCESS WILL BE YOURS.
– PURE AND SIMPLE

BY THINKHARD KIPPLING (RUDYARDS SMARTER BROTHER)

So, the Pies have it, final thoughts...

This is the end of the beginning. Hopefully I've convinced you that the pies have it. They have the knowledge, wisdom, know-how, insights, pain and more that you need. When you combine your people with the rigorous Strategic Thinking process you'll make an amazing game-changing business.

Theory is great. But theory doesn't build businesses. Better questions leading to better thinking and better execution builds great businesses.

- If you need to reread this book, do it. This book is like a Strategic Thinking manual or guide, not something to read once and forget about. The videos in www.piesorpiecharts.com are there for you to use and share with your team and colleagues. I do believe that the formula I've adopted for this book is unique. I wanted to produce something that really genuinely helps the reader, by combining:Easy to understand, plain-speaking text. Making the complex simple, not the other way around as so many authors seem to do.
- Easy to follow illustrations to reinforce the points.
- A series of explainer videos setting the context of each chapter and key steps.

The Strategic Thinking process has been delivered across the world by DPI Partners for circa 40 years. Internationally, we have worked with some brilliant organisations such as; 3M, FedEx, DPD, Shell, Leica, Unilever, Caterpillar, McGrawHill, St John Ambulance, Willis, and many, many more. We've also worked with some relatively unknown smaller but very special businesses such as Freedom Group, BB&A, CBW, Soprema, Distech Controls, Harbor Solutions, Arena, ZigZag and many more amazing companies. In fact, we have helped well over 3500 businesses of all sizes globally, profit and non-profit, to outthink, outpace and outmanoeuvre their competition.

In the time between starting this book and finishing it, I've rebranded DPI Europe. I've blended it into a business I co-founded in 2018 with three awesome entrepreneurs – peer2peer. Peer2peer is for business leaders, executives, owner entrepreneurs and SMEs who are passionate about living their best life and building exceptional businesses and teams. We're dedicating the next 10 years to changing the game in the coaching world. All four of us were increasingly alarmed at what was happening with expensive, lazy, stale and largely ineffective franchised coaching models. The founders of these coaching businesses may have started off with good intent, but, somewhere along the journey, they lost sight of the client. They shifted the gun-sight to becoming a recruiter of "corporate refugees" (this is a phrase coined and trademarked by the world's greatest accountant Derek Blair). They are only interested in finding recently made redundant middle managers and convincing them to part with $60k and $3k/month thereafter for their "consultancy in a box". They're flooding the market promising 30x growth…

I'll step off my soapbox now.

In Europe, DPI's great critical thinking material is now branded "Torque" within the growing peer2peer family. It remains all about working with SLTs to help them improve both their thinking and the effectiveness of their businesses. We help them to get things running more effectively and efficiently.

Our tagline #LoveYourFlight says it all. Running a great business starts by involving your extended SLT to do some proper Strategic Thinking. Get this right and you will be successful and, in turn, Love Your Flight.

Our thriving peer2peer movement is:

- Encouraged to ***Be Bold***
- Enabled to ***Be Balanced***
- Empowered to ***Be Brilliant***

This is not the entirety of the peer2peer service, of course. This is only the Strategic Thinking part. We've shed loads of other frameworks, formats and focus tools to help our growing community:

- Innovation frames – Touchpoint Analysis and Stealth Threat will feature in my **Book #2 – "CrADLE"**. Now that I've navigated my way through writing and publishing a book it hopefully won't take me the 4 years this one did ;-) At its heart is that innovation is most effective by both looking from the ***outside in*** and the ***inside out***
- **Book #3 – Capability Compass**. Will focus on the 8 capabilities SLTs and entrepreneurs need to master in order to build great businesses.

Finally, the real inspiration behind the book title. During lockdown one i.e. between March and May 2020, I, like so many middle-aged blokes with kids trapped within the confines of our castle, ate, drank and snacked like never before. It's fair to say I stacked on a bit of extra timber. Then, when we were allowed to go around to other households as long as we stayed outside and didn't have more than six people, we played darts at Senny's house. During a break from my appalling darts, I shared the news that I'm going to write a book about Strategic Thinking. Quick as a flash Steve (ironically, a short chubby fella himself) said, "What are you going to call it, Pies or Pie charts?" When the laughter subsided, I thought to myself, actually, that's not a bad idea. I then came up with the rationale introduced to you in the opening chapter.

I'm pleased to report that in the ensuing six months I lost over 10 kilos through abstaining from snacking, drinking at home and eating after 7pm.

If you would like to contact me directly, for any reason, I can be reached through the piesorpiecharts.com website.

If you enjoyed this book, I would love it if you would give it a review.

* 9 7 8 1 9 1 4 1 5 1 5 7 6 *
BV - #0084 - 191125 - C0 - 246/189/11 - PB - 9781914151576 - Matt Lamination